9-20-23

AMERICAN PATRIOTIC AND POLITICAL CHINA

BY MARIAN KLAMKIN

White House China

*American Patriotic and
Political China*

BY MARIAN KLAMKIN

AMERICAN PATRIOTIC AND POLITICAL CHINA

CHARLES SCRIBNER'S SONS
NEW YORK

Designed by Peter Landa

1 3 7 9 11 13 15 17 19 MD/C 20 18 16 14 12 10 8 6 4 2

Color printed in Japan
Text and black and white illustrations printed in the United States of America
Library of Congress Catalog Card Number 72-6557
SBN 684-13182-X

CONTENTS

T 1764326

ACKNOWLEDGMENTS

I owe a deep debt of gratitude for the help I received on this book to the following people: Herbert R. Collins, curator in charge, division of political history, Smithsonian Institution, Washington, D.C.; Dr. Edmund B. Sullivan, resident curator, DeWitt collection, University of Hartford, Hartford, Connecticut; Mr. William H. Watkins, director, Mattatuck Museum, Waterbury, Connecticut; and Mr. and Mrs. Leon Weissel, Fort Lee, New Jersey.

I would also like to thank Mrs. Mary Moorcroft, assistant public relations manager, Josiah Wedgwood and Sons Limited, for sending photographs, and my husband, Charles Klamkin, for taking photographs.

1

INTRODUCTION

Since ancient times the surfaces of pottery and porcelain have been used by the potter to express his messages for posterity. The Greeks made vases that were given as prizes at their games, inscribed with such legends as "I am a prize from Athens." Other presentation vases that still exist today tell us that "The boy is handsome," or ask "O Father Jove, may I be rich?" On still another vase the message that "Hippokritos is the most handsome" can be found.

The soft clay of unfired vases, cups, plates, tiles, tablets, and urns has long been considered a suitable place where the potter could express some written sentiment of his own or of the person for whom the pot was being made. Many potters, centuries before it became customary to mark the bottom of a ceramic object to identify its maker, were satisfied simply to establish themselves as the creators of the objects that were to outlive them and of which they were so proud. Often they let the vases or urns speak for themselves. "Exekias it was who made and painted me" is found on one such vase.

Medieval potters also left us messages on vases and plates. A large jug in the Victoria and Albert Museum has the interesting inscription "Master Baldem Menniken, Potter, Dwelling in Rorren [Germany], I submit to God's will. Patience under suffering." This was a political statement made during a period of religious and political struggle in Europe. Politics, religion, patriotism, and morality have long been subjects for ceramic decoration.

In Elizabethan times in England, potters made stove tiles and other ceramic objects with the royal initials and bearing the Tudor rose and the arms of England and France. By the seventeenth century, many British potters were signing their wares, not on the bottom surfaces where they wouldn't easily be seen, but as part of the decoration of the object. A large three-handled posset pot in the

British Museum carries this inscription, "God bless the Queen and Prence Gorg^e. Drink and be mery and mary. B. B. John Meir made this cup 1708." British potters of the early eighteenth century are better remembered for their potting ability and patriotic spirit than they are for their spelling.

By the time of the American Revolution British potters were not quite as patriotic, and they established a lucrative trade with America by siding with the colonists' cause in the struggle for independence.

Late seventeenth- and early eighteenth-century ceramics made by the British can be found with valentine messages as inscriptions. A three-handled jug in the British Museum has these words inscribed on it, "Ann Draper this cup I made for you and so no more. J. W. 1707." A triangular stand of earthenware, probably part of a tombstone, still has this inscription:

1695

E.E.

WHEN THIS V. C.

REMEMBER MEE

In the days of the artisan-potter each piece of clay that was formed into a vessel was the personal expression of the individual potter. Often, when made to order for a particular customer, the product would be individualized in shape or decoration to suit the client's taste.

When the British pottery industry became mechanized, beginning with the firm founded in 1759 by Josiah Wedgwood, ceramics were decorated to order for the market for which they were intended. Wedgwood, by the invention and utilization of machinery and mass-production methods, ended the era of the artisan-potter in England. Identical objects could be manufactured in large quantity, and the decoration, still applied by hand, had to be acceptable not just to one customer but to an entire market. However, the practice of designing a special plate, pitcher, or other object for a client who might commit for a quantity of one design continued. To this day plates and other ceramic objects are decorated to order for American customers, and it is customary for British as well as American potters to make and decorate objects of clay to celebrate national or local anniversaries, to commemorate national heroes or events, to express political slogans, or to promote candidates or political parties. National symbols and landmarks are also subjects for this type of commemorative china.

British potters, from the very beginning of their dealings with American cus-

Fig. 1 Left Many Liverpool creamware jugs made for the American market had prints of the American eagle under the lip. This eagle is somwhat more fierce in appearance than most. (MATTATUCK MUSEUM. PHOTOGRAPH BY CHARLES KLAMKIN)

Fig. 2 Right With the invention of a method for printing on pottery, customers monograms could be applied at little cost. The monogram and American eagle are printed under the lip of this creamware jug. (MATTATUCK MUSEUM. PHOTOGRAPH BY CHARLES KLAMKIN)

tomers, seemed to display far more sentiment for the continuing, lucrative trade abroad than they did for their own country's cause in the American struggle for independence. Many of Josiah Wedgwood's products and those of other British potters made for shipment abroad in the latter part of the eighteenth century clearly show the potters' support of the colonists' cause. Portrait medallions of American patriots were among Wedgwood's earliest successful efforts in his newly developed jasperware and basalt. George Washington, Benjamin Franklin, and other patriots were immortalized on Wedgwood portrait medallions, and there was a ready market in America for these items.

The Wedgwood firm's contribution to the American ceramics market has been enormous and will be discussed separately in Chapter 6. Wedgwood was as good a businessman as he was a potter, and his expertise in making and marketing wares for shipment abroad was for the time extremely advanced. Other British potters, encouraged by Wedgwood's example, made and decorated ceramics that would appeal to Americans following the War of 1812. It is interesting that jugs, mugs, and plates with printed and painted motifs, poems, portraits, and sentiments that might have been considered treasonable to the British cause at the beginning of the nineteenth century were nevertheless made in large quantity by British potters for their American customers.

During this period of struggle between the two nations, and with many interruptions in trade due to embargoes and difficulty in direct shipping to America, the potters of Staffordshire and Liverpool did not concern themselves so much with the quality of their goods as with their usefulness and with the patriotic appeal the decoration of their wares had for the American market. By this time British potters had found a method to cheaply and uniformly decorate earthenware by use of printing, and handwork in decoration could be kept to a minimum.

Hand-painting was sometimes employed over the printing on these inexpensive tablewares and presentation pieces, but this type of decoration did not require the work of talented artists. Enameling over a printed design required only that the decorator stay somewhat within the printed lines. Cheaper wares were produced that had no hand-decorating whatsoever but simply printed decoration in sepia or black. The technique of applying decoration to earthenware by means of inked transfers made from copperplates will be discussed in Chapter 3, but it should be kept in mind that this technique, simple and cheap to use, made it possible for the Staffordshire and Liverpool potters to manufacture and decorate in quantity earthenware that appealed strongly to the patriotism of Americans. This market for British wares has been important to the British pottery industry for over two hundred years.

In the latter part of the eighteenth century Wedgwood looked on the American market as unique. He did not consider it as a place to trade in his more expensive decorative wares. These were marketed in England, France, Germany, and other European countries. He did not judge America ripe for expensive things during his lifetime, and at the time of his death, in 1795, the situation had not changed to any extent. Wedgwood had sent mainly cheap goods and seconds, which sold in quantity to those American customers in need of teaware and plates to replace their more primitive woodenware and pewter. Post-Revolutionary War newspapers, published in Boston and other American cities, advertised the arrival

Fig. 3 Unusual eagle placement on front of Liverpool jug. The print is not as skillfully rendered as those in Figures 1 and 2. (MATTATUCK MUSEUM. PHOTOGRAPH BY CHARLES KLAMKIN)

of "Queen's ware teacups" and other useful ceramic objects. It was not until the middle of the nineteenth century that Americans could afford the more decorative and expensive products of the British pottery industry in quantity.

The earliest examples of pottery made and decorated in England expressly for the American market are the cream colored jugs, mugs, and punch bowls printed or painted (or both) with American motifs. This creamware, frequently referred to in early advertisements in American newspapers as "yellow ware," was at first decorated in the city of Liverpool and shipped from that seaport during the periods at the beginning of the nineteenth century when trade was continued between Great Britain and America.

Some of this ware was manufactured as well as decorated in Liverpool potteries, and those made at the Herculaneum Pottery of that city are among the few marked specimens of this type of ware. Wedgwood and other Staffordshire potters made this lead-glazed, cream colored earthenware, but few of these pieces are marked by their makers. All this kind of early printed Anglo-American creamware is referred to as "Liverpool ware."

Wedgwood, who was England's leading potter during the latter half of the eighteenth century, strongly and rather openly supported American independence, and corresponded with Benjamin Franklin on the subject. He also contributed money for the relief of American prisoners held in England during the revolution. Wedgwood designed and manufactured in quantity intaglio seals in basalt and jasper with the motif of the coiled rattlesnake and the legend "Don't Tread on Me." This seal was first made in 1777 and was distributed among American sympathizers in England. Many seals were also sent to this country. The motif used was derived from the flag flown by John Paul Jones of the American fleet.

The rattlesnake medallion was set into many types of jewelry. Those sympathetic with the American cause wore the seal set into shoe buckles, buttons, belt buckles, brooches, and rings. Snuffboxes also were made with the seal set into the lids. During this period of Wedgwood production, Wedgwood and his partner, William Bentley, marked all the objects in basalt and jasper that left their factory. The rattlesnake medallion and an antislavery medallion were exceptions, however.

While Wedgwood was probably the first of the British potters to realize that there was tremendous potential in future trade with America, there were many others who followed Wedgwood's example and established good will with their customers abroad during the period of conflict. After Wedgwood's death other potters capitalized on this idea to design patriotic ceramics for the American

Fig. 4 "Success to America" was only one of the unpatriotic sentiments expressed by British potters in their attempt to capture the American pottery market early in the nineteenth century. (MATTA-TUCK MUSEUM. PHOTOGRAPH BY CHARLES KLAMKIN)

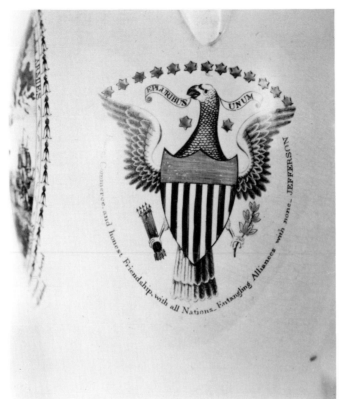

Fig. 5 Left *A variety of eagles can be found under the lips of many of the Liverpool jugs made for the American market. This one is enameled in yellow, red, and blue. Fig. 6 Right Unusual hand-decorated Liverpool jug with picture of American ship. Flag is painted in yellow and blue. Masonic emblems adorn sides. Floral border around rim.* (MATTATUCK MUSEUM. PHOTOGRAPH BY CHARLES KLAMKIN)

market. By this time, the Wedgwood firm, under the ownership of Wedgwood's son, Josiah II, was committed to making many expensive, decorative objects in addition to the cheaper, useful tablewares, but few of these were manufactured expressly for the American market, even though such Wedgwood wares were purchased here.

Rather than attempt to sell expensive plates to the citizens of a struggling young nation, many of the British potters developed a cheap earthenware that could be inexpensively decorated with American scenes and motifs. These sold in quantity in the first half of the nineteenth century. To a country that had been unable to establish a ceramics industry of any note, the white earthenware with motifs of familiar landmarks, patriotic symbols, and scenes had extremely strong appeal. Dark blue printed ware was very popular for a long time, and the views to be found on these plates are, in many cases, the only evidence that we

7

have of how our buildings, cities, and natural wonders looked during the first part of the nineteenth century.

Portraits of patriots and slogans for freedom can also be found on many of these plates, printed in a shade of deep blue that seemed only to appeal to Americans. It is not known why dark blue was popular only on this continent, but the blue and white printed plates made for sale in England at the same time are of a much lighter hue. The market for dark blue and white printed ware lasted until about 1850, when the fashion for other colors or for plain white dinnerware became the vogue for middle-class Americans.

Plates and other ceramic objects have been used as expressions of patriotic and political sentiments since we became an independent nation. The men, the symbols, and the causes that have all been a part of American history for the past two hundred years have also been subjects for pottery shape or decoration. Specially decorated plates have been made to raise money for patriotic and political causes, and this custom continues to this day. In many cases, the objects are still supplied by the potters of Great Britain.

With very few exceptions, most of the patriotic and political china that has been made is of poor quality from the ceramicist's point of view. The event, the place, the person, or the cause the object represents has been reason enough for Americans to preserve and collect this type of decorated china. While political figures may once have been controversial, they are usually represented on china decoration with dignity and restraint. Therefore, there are few caricatures of political figures to be found on pottery or porcelain.

The styles and methods of plate decoration may have changed somewhat in 200 years. However, the custom of immortalizing political candidates and statesmen on pottery and porcelain continues. Two hundred years of American history can be traced on the ceramic objects that represent political campaigns, historical events, places, people, causes, and symbols of the United States. Traditionally, the British potters still provide us with the best of these objects. Other plates and ceramics decorated with patriotic and political motifs are now supplied by American potters or are made elsewhere. American collectors and historians, who have long had a high regard for the patriotic and political mementos of our past, have always considered the quality of the message more important than the medium on which it appears.

2

CHINESE EXPORT FOR THE AMERICAN MARKET

While the shapes and decoration of objects made of pottery and porcelain are of primary interest in this book, it is important to know where the ideas for colors and styles in these wares originally came from. The credit for white ware decorated in blue and for the use of patriotic motifs on china can be given to the Chinese, who introduced those types of porcelain to the West during the Ch'ien Lung period (1736–1796). During this "golden age of Chinese porcelain," plates were decorated to order for foreign markets with coats-of-arms and patriotic motifs. Following the founding of the American Republic and the establishment of direct trade with China, plates were made that were enameled with pictures of American clipper ships flying the new flag. The wingspread eagle was another popular center motif for plates of this vintage.

The use of blue enamel as plate decoration goes back much further than the last quarter of the eighteenth century, however. For many years plates decorated at Canton in China bore Oriental scenes that covered the entire surface of the plates. At first British and Dutch potters copied these Oriental scenes, and later, when the printing process was used for plate decoration, the Staffordshire potters continued using the blue on white earthenware to depict scenes that would appeal to Americans.

It is interesting to note that quite early in the history of china collecting in America the Chinese tea and dinnerware that was imported here was called by the name "Lowestoft." Writers on the subject were aware that this was a misnomer, but no effort on their part, or on the part of later writers, has been able to abolish this label. Antique dealers, museum curators, and collectors are

Fig. 7 Chinese-made porcelain for export to America had patriotic motifs. This is a stylized eagle with spread wings. (SMITHSONIAN INSTITUTION. PHOTOGRAPH BY CHARLES KLAMKIN)

aware that none of this porcelain originated in England, but was imported by the East India Company at first, and later brought directly to American ports when American-Chinese trade was established. However, Lowestoft is the name that has stuck. Occasionally "Chinese export" is used instead.

The china thus misnamed bears armorial motifs, monograms, and ciphers, and although it is bordered with polychrome flowers that appear to be European in nature, the ware and the decoration are Chinese. The decoration was designed to appeal to Western tastes, and much of it became the prototype for china made elsewhere at a later date.

There are in existence today copies of orders for plates, tea sets, and other items from China, and ship invoices that record the delivery of specially decorated porcelain for customers in the United States. George Washington owned several sets of china that were decorated to order for him with patriotic motifs. One of these is the famous "Cincinnati" service, with the figure of Fame holding the Order of the Cincinnati in the center of the plates.

The Chinese were extremely conscientious and obliging when it came to filling special orders for plate decoration. There are many stories told about the carefully written instructions that were sent along with a drawing to be placed on the center of plates. When the instructions were written on the same piece of paper as the drawing, they were often repeated in enamel in the center of each plate, along with the desired coat-of-arms or monogram.

Following the Revolution, and with the opening of direct trade with China, the person ordering a set of chinaware could design his own pattern, and many patriotic motifs were used. These were all one-of-a-kind services, and a bride could wait two years before the clipper ship returned that bore her new plates. It was at this time, however, that American clipper ships and eagles replaced the British-looking floral borders and center motifs. Frequently, the old traditional borders were used, and the center motif was added.

Social, fraternal, and military clubs, organized at the end of the eighteenth and the beginning of the nineteenth century, ordered punch bowls and plates with their special insignias on them. Often, specific members ordered these same objects with personal monograms added. Frequently, these personalized china objects were given to officers of the group as tokens of their fellows' esteem.

3

LIVERPOOL
PRINTED WARE

Without doubt the most desirable of all patriotic china with designs relating to American history are the so-called Liverpool jugs, mugs, and punch bowls made by British potters at Liverpool and elsewhere in England expressly for the American market during the first quarter of the nineteenth century. These pieces were advertised in American seaport newspapers as "yellow" or "cream" ware and were designed to appeal to American sentiment or patriotism. Ships that took part in the naval battles of the War of 1812, prominent Americans and American military events of the period, best wishes for the development of American trade and industry, and homage to particular localities are the categories of subjects that were at first painted, and later printed, on the cream colored ware. The most desirable of objects in this category are those that were both printed and hand-enameled in color over the glaze.

Although some of these cream colored wares were made in Liverpool, many were manufactured in the Staffordshire section of England, which, by the nineteenth century, was already established as the center of the developing ceramics industry in England. Wedgwood, Leeds, and other companies made the cylindrical, handled mugs and the melon-shaped pitchers (or jugs) that were smooth enough and plain enough to adapt readily to printed decorative motifs. The tall jugs with the slightly bulging centers were early advertised as "Liverpool jugs" because all were at first sent to that city for the application of printed designs.

The technique for decorating pottery by transfer printing was discovered by a Liverpool printer, John Sadler, who opened an establishment at 14 Harrington Street in 1748. He later took Guy Green as a partner, and the firm was still

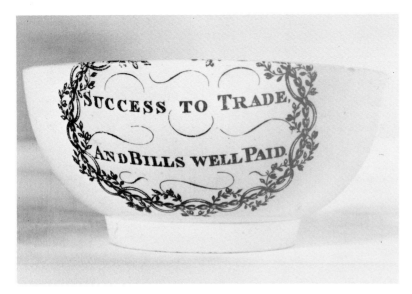

Fig. 8 British potters used transfers designed for jug shapes on punch bowls and, less frequently, on plates and other objects. Printed in black on creamware, this bowl expresses the British tradesman's sentiment that hostilities would eventually be forgotten and trade with America reestablished. (MATTATUCK MUSEUM. PHOTOGRAPH BY CHARLES KLAMKIN)

Fig. 9 Just about all the American patriotic symbols the British engraver could think of are incorporated into the print on this jug. Washington, Columbia, the liberty cap, the eagle, the flag, Benjamin Franklin, and the map of America make this one of the most patriotic of all our early jugs. Ca. 1815. (MATTATUCK MUSEUM. PHOTOGRAPH BY CHARLES KLAMKIN)

in business in 1799. If we remember that all pottery was decorated by hand before the discovery of transfer printing, it will become obvious that this discovery was a remarkable boon to the pottery industry in England. The process was a simple one. Sadler printed an image on paper with an ordinary copper or steel plate. He then laid the wet print on the glazed pottery object, pressed it, and later burned it in. By this means a number of objects could be decorated with identical transfers, and the work required only that the artist engrave the original plate. Most of the early printed decorations were done in black ink, but there are a few to be found that were printed in blue or vermilion. The most highly prized of the early printed creamware is the kind that was partly enameled by hand over the printing. Since only lines had to be filled in with solid, usually unshaded, colors, this did not require the work of skilled artists either, and local women and children were hired to enamel pottery.

The advantages of printed decoration for pottery were many. The cost could be kept to a minimum, thereby enabling the British potters to compete favorably with Dutch tile makers for that part of the market. The wares that were made in Staffordshire could be shipped directly to Liverpool, decorated over the glaze, and then shipped directly to America or elsewhere without being sent back to Staffordshire for further glazing or firing. A considerable amount of expense could be saved on breakage alone by avoiding this extra packing and transporting. Since the discovery of the transfer printing process had proved so valuable for the Sadler and Green firm, no patent was taken out by the partners to save them from having to describe publicly their process. However, it was such a simple procedure that others soon went into the business of printing on pottery, among the earliest the firm of Hancock and Holdship. Some of the Staffordshire potters soon hired their own engravers, who designed their own transfer prints.

Besides the tall jugs, punch bowls in a variety of sizes, and the previously mentioned cylindrical drinking mugs were shapes that were easily adapted to the transfer designs. Plates, teapots, and other shapes were also printed, but few had patriotic motifs for the American market. From the number of jugs in various sizes that exist today, it is obvious that the jug shape was the one most often produced.

While Sadler and Green recognized the futility of attempting to protect their discovery and competition had become strong for their type of work, the firm of Josiah Wedgwood still continued to use the services of the Sadler and Green firm long after many Staffordshire potters had started to do their own printing.

Fig. 10 Left Washington, depicted with his foot on the head of the conquered British lion, was a motif that should have been considered treasonous by the British pottery decorator. Printed in black. Fig. 11 Right Prints of portraits of Samuel Adams and John Hancock adorn this Washington jug. (MATTATUCK MUSEUM. PHOTOGRAPH BY CHARLES KLAMKIN)

It is interesting that the Liverpool printers only lasted in business a few years following the death of Josiah Wedgwood.

William Adams of Cobridge is said to have introduced the process of printing on creamware to the Staffordshire region around 1775, and other potters followed his example. Since so few of the jugs are marked by their makers it is almost impossible to determine their origin. However, some of the engravings are signed by the Staffordshire artists, which is further proof that not all the printing was done in Liverpool. Among these artists were F. Morris and T. Fletcher of Shelton and Machin of Burslem.

John Sadler's process of printing decorations on pottery was an important development of the British industrial revolution. Staffordshire potters were turning out in quantity like objects for markets at home and abroad and the ability to decorate these objects in an identical manner without having to employ trained artists was an enormous advantage. Pitchers could be printed to order and even monogrammed for a particular sea captain or other client in very little time. Combination prints of historically related subjects could be chosen by the customer, and the jugs packed and ready for shipment by the time the ship was ready to leave the port of Liverpool.

The majority of Liverpool jugs seem to have been made for the American market between 1815 and 1820. These were brought into this country by clipper ship and advertised and sold in American seaports. The one scholarly attempt to categorize the number of transfer etchings made expressly for the American market can be found in *Liverpool Transfer Designs on Anglo–American Pottery*, a book written by Robert H. McCauley in 1942. McCauley lists 265 different transfers. The prints were used interchangeably on the wares of many potters, and the existence of a particular transfer on a marked piece does not necessarily mean that all wares with the same transfer were made by that one potter. In addition, the transfers were used in many combinations, and frequently the transfer on one side of a jug will have no relationship to the design on the other, except that they are American motifs. Many of the portraits of American patriots were adapted from contemporary engravings of paintings that could be found in books of the period.

Obviously, the spirit of trade loomed larger in the breasts of the British potters and decorators during the War of 1812 than did the spirits of patriotism and sentiment. The engravers showed a rather scanty knowledge of the American heroes that they used for subject matter, but certainly they understood the reverence in which these American heros were held by their countrymen. Nor was a great deal of attention given to historical accuracy in the printed decoration. On some of the early pitchers, the chain motif with the names of the states then settled in America are more source of amusement than an accurate depiction of American geography at the time. The name of "Kentuckey" was often substituted for Rhode Island, "Tenasee" was included as a state before it became one, and "Boston" was frequently used in place of Massachusetts.

A great many of the engraved designs to be found on Liverpool ware are related to the death of George Washington. "He in Glory, America in Tears" is

Fig. 12 Left *White House in Washington. Made by Enoch Wood & Sons.* (MATTATUCK MUSEUM. PHOTOGRAPH BY CHARLES KLAMKIN). *Fig. 13* Right *Souvenir plate, printed in blue, of Washington's headquarters in Newburgh, New York.* (MATTATUCK MUSEUM. PHOTOGRAPH BY CHARLES KLAMKIN)

a common lament on many of these jugs. "A Man without Example, a Patriot without Reproach" is used in conjunction with Washington's portrait and sentimental renderings of Washington's tomb. Other funereal symbols usually accompany these prints. The engravers also wished "Success to America whose Militia is better than standing Armies."

Besides Washington, portraits of Jefferson, Adams, and Franklin are found on Liverpool wares. Figures of Justice and Liberty are often seen, and early British impressions of the American eagle were also used as decorative motifs. The British potters wished "Success to [American-British] Trade" and obviously felt no patriotic compunctions about picturing George Washington standing with one foot upon the head of the defeated British lion. American merchant ships were often pictured with billowing sails. Jugs depicting naval battles of the War of 1812 will be treated separately, since these are an especially interesting category of decoration and are, for the most part, historically accurate.

If the engravers took artistic license with American subject matter, so did some of the artists who filled in the lines with overglaze enamel coloring. The American flag was sometimes painted in with whatever colors were available at the time. On at least one printed and painted pitcher, the flag is pictured as having the stars on a yellow ground, and the stripes have been filled in with solid blue.

On other pitchers sails are filled with wind blowing from one direction while flags have their own mysterious breezes coming from the opposite direction. While these motifs must have amused the sailors who purchased pitchers in Liverpool to take home as souvenirs of their voyages, it did not seem to deter them from giving the historical jugs places of honor in their homes. Many of the remaining jugs have been carefully cared for by generations of heirs of these early American merchant seamen.

Alice Morse Earle wrote in 1892 that "china collectors find in America more, cheaper, and more varied specimens of Liverpool wares, especially those bearing transfer prints, than can be found in England." She continued, "They [Liverpool jugs] abound in American antique shops. Even the rarest and most interesting of all, prints on tiles, pitchers and teapots bearing the mark of Sadler [the Liverpool printer]—are often discovered here." This, of course, is no longer true. Most of the Liverpool pitchers and other objects with American printed motifs have long since found their way into museums, especially those in East Coast seaport towns. However, it is the attention given by writers like Mrs. Earle to this originally mass-produced, cheap ware that has been responsible for the existence of the fine collections of Liverpool ware in this country today.

4

BLUE AND WHITE
HISTORICAL CHINA

Although the British potters of the Staffordshire region enjoyed a lucrative trade with America before and immediately following the Revolutionary War, during the period between 1808 and 1814 little direct trade was carried on between the two countries. This hiatus was caused by the Napoleonic wars between Britain and France, which involved commercial as well as military hostilities. In 1807 the British demanded duty from American ships that were trading with countries from which British trade was excluded. The United States then issued an embargo forbidding Americans to trade with Britain or France. The long embargo was harmful to the economy of the United States as well as to the economies of countries against which it was issued. Although it was difficult to enforce, the embargo did cut down British export trade, and potters suffered terrible reverses. It is not surprising that Liverpool pitchers can be found today with cartoons commemorating "The Long Embargo."

By the end of the War of 1812 and the hostilities with France, the British potters were extremely anxious to resume trade with America. This is one of the reasons why so many pro-American motifs can be found on the Liverpool ware of the period. Nationalistic feelings in America ran high enough to convince the British potters that any wares with American scenes, patriots' portraits, and other motifs that would appeal to American chauvinism would find a ready market. Many new industries were being established. The new country was expanding rapidly, and there were a great many Americans who could now afford to replace their old pewter and woodenware with plates and other ceramic objects that were more up to date.

Fig. 14 The Baltimore and Ohio Railroad. Printed in dark blue. Made by Enoch Wood. (MATTATUCK MUSEUM. PHOTOGRAPH BY CHARLES KLAMKIN)

Fig. 15 The Baltimore and Ohio Railroad shown on an inclined plane. Printed in dark blue. Made by Enoch Wood. (MATTATUCK MUSEUM. PHOTOGRAPH BY CHARLES KLAMKIN)

Fig. 16 Castle Garden, Battery, New York. Printed in dark blue. Made by Enoch Wood. (MATTATUCK MUSEUM. PHOTOGRAPH BY CHARLES KLAMKIN)

Fig. 17 *A more complete view of Castle Garden can be found on this Enoch Wood platter printed in dark blue.* (MATTATUCK MUSEUM. PHOTOGRAPH BY CHARLES KLAMKIN)

Fig. 18 *Table Rock and Niagara Falls. Printed in dark blue. Made by Enoch Wood.* (MATTATUCK MUSEUM. PHOTOGRAPH BY CHARLES KLAMKIN)

Since direct trade with China was now a privilege that American shippers could engage in without interference from the European countries, the ware made by the British for the American market had to be cheaper than the Chinese export pottery and porcelain and had to be decorated to appeal to American taste. A popular kind of ware that was cheap and very appealing was being shipped out of Canton, China, to America. This china was white with all-over patterns in blue. In their attempt to compete with the Chinese market, the Staffordshire potters looked to the Chinese for the prototypes of the teaware and dinnerware that they sent to the United States. The Chinese ware had rural Oriental scenes and buildings familiar only to the Chinese plate decorators. The British went further and found scenes depicting American life for their plate decoration.

At first, however, the British potters decorated plates with almost exact copies of the Chinese scenes. From the beginning this so-called Willow ware was very successful on the American market. The use of scenes of American cities and

Fig. 19 View of New York from Brooklyn Heights. From painting by G. Wall. Printed in dark blue. Made by A. Stevenson. (MATTATUCK MUSEUM. PHOTOGRAPH BY CHARLES KLAMKIN)

towns, new public buildings and other landmarks, portraits of patriots, and coats-of-arms of individual states were a Western attempt to give the American customer more what he really wanted. The British blue and white plates were very cheap to make, costing only a few cents apiece.

While the Liverpool pitchers, mugs, and punch bowls were mainly cream colored, the cheap dinnerware was printed in blue on white china. The blue, a deep indigo that was made exclusively for Americans, took better on a white glaze, and the contrast was thought to be more attractive. White china was in demand and was made with the blue print in imitation of the Chinese plates and of the Dutch Delft that had earlier been seen in America. The blue printing was easy to use on the cheap white earthenware made in Staffordshire and covered a multitude of imperfections. The density of color and the variety of shading possible covered blisters in the glaze and marks left from the clay cockspurs that were used to separate the plates in the kiln. If the subject matter of the decoration was an image of the "immortal Washington" or the Boston State House in all its bucolic splendor, Americans would hardly notice that the surfaces of the plates were bumpy.

There were few British potters who did not produce blue and white printed ware for the American market. Great quantities of tableware were shipped from Burslem, Stoke-upon-Trent, Cobridge, Hanley, Tunstall, and Liverpool. Some of the plates were marked by the maker and others can be definitely attributed to a particular potter. Many others, however, cannot be identified.

Border designs on many of the unmarked blue and white historical plates are often a key to the manufacturer. The central motifs were frequently copied from illustrated books and sold by the engraver to various potters. Border devices seem to have been the property of individual potters and were not often exchanged. A great variety of border motifs was used. Flowers, seashells, leaves, vines, birds, fruit, and various scroll patterns were popular. On certain plates and platters, portraits of American patriots are intertwined in the border patterns, while related motifs are used in the center. The American eagle and stars are other border motifs that the potters thought suitable for decorating plates for the American market.

Many of the views to be found on the old blue and white plates were reproduced from an illustrated book entitled *The Beauties of America*. English tourists brought back sketches of the wonders that they saw in America, and these, too, were copied and adapted for plate decoration. In many cases the potters them-

Fig. 20 *The White House, with cows in foreground. Printed in dark blue. Made by Enoch Wood.* (MATTATUCK MUSEUM. PHOTOGRAPH BY CHARLES KLAMKIN)

Fig. 21 *New York City Hall. Printed in dark blue. Made by Ridgway.* (MATTATUCK MUSEUM. PHOTOGRAPH BY CHARLES KLAMKIN)

Fig. 22 *Arms of New York. Printed in dark blue. Made by T. Mayer.* (MATTATUCK MUSEUM. PHOTOGRAPH BY CHARLES KLAMKIN)

Fig. 23 Columbia College. Printed in dark blue. Made by R. S. W. (MAT-TATUCK MUSEUM. PHOTOTRAPH BY CHARLES KLAMKIN)

Fig. 24 American Museum (Scudder's), New York. Printed in dark blue. Made by R. S. W. (MATTATUCK MUSEUM. PHOTOGRAPH BY CHARLES KLAMKIN)

Fig. 25 Boston Hospital. Printed in dark blue. Made by Ralph Stevenson. (MATTATUCK MUSEUM. PHOTOGRAPH BY CHARLES KLAMKIN)

selves went to the expense of sending representatives to America for the purpose of bringing back drawings and paintings of the latest architecture, new monuments, and scenic wonders. The most recent methods of transportation, such as the steamboat and the railroad, were also appealing subjects for plate decoration. The newly invented "camera-obscura" was used to record scenes for adaptation as plate engravings. Many adaptations of the seal of the United States adorned popular dinnerware in the first half of the nineteenth century.

As long as it was American, no scene or motif was felt to be unsuitable for blue plate decoration. Almshouses, prisons, warehouses, and deaf and dumb asylums were considered to be as suitable for decoration as churches, ships, inns, and colleges. The Philadelphia Waterworks Building, designed by Benjamin Latrobe, does look just as handsome and majestic as the White House in the center of a Staffordshire plate.

Not only everyday scenes but historical and imaginative ones, such as "The Landing of the Pilgrims" or "George Washington on the Lawn in Front of the Mansion at Mount Vernon," were dreamed up by the Staffordshire artists. The "Battle of Bunker Hill" was re-fought on more than one vegetable dish or teapot. In all, more than 250 different historical views were designed for the British potters, and these plates were sold in enormous quantity in America between the years 1815 and 1830.

As the printing methods of the British potters became more sophisticated, multicolored printed plates came into use. Green, sepia, chocolate, pink, black, and mulberry color were used. In addition, the blue and white plates made between 1830 and 1850 were of a lighter hue, the dark blue having gone out of fashion by then. At the time of the American centennial there were few American potters who could yet give the British any strong competition for the bulk of the American trade in table ceramics. Many of the secrets necessary to produce cheap earthenware in quantity were well kept in England, and the British potters made it very difficult for their master workmen to emigrate to America to work for the few potteries that were being established there. By the middle of the nineteenth century, the secret of manufacturing acceptable plates at a very low price and decorating them to American taste had still not been learned in America. The few British potters who came to this country were not, as we shall see later, very successful. The clay, wood, and coal, and the methods of transportation necessary for success in the pottery industry, were easily accessible. Skilled workmen were not.

5

THE STAFFORDSHIRE POTTERS

Because many of the blue and white plates made for the American market in England were not marked, it is often just by the border designs alone that we can identify the makers. Some of the center decorations on the blue and white plates were peculiar to just one potter, but often we can find marked plates from two different potters with the same center motif.

Probably the earliest Staffordshire potter to make printed plates in dark blue exclusively for export to America was Enoch Wood. The son of Ralph Wood, also a potter, Enoch was born on January 31, 1759. The younger Wood enjoyed a long career in the pottery industry and probably saw it change a great deal. Wood himself produced wares that he felt would appeal to his American customers, and an early creamware bust of George Washington is attributed to him. It is probably the earliest Staffordshire bust made of our first president. It is also thought that some of the printed pitchers commemorating our naval heroes of the War of 1812 were made by Wood's firm. Wood went into his own business in 1783, and in 1790 he took James Caldwell as a partner. The firm was known as Wood and Caldwell until 1792, when it became Enoch Wood & Co. In 1818 it became Enoch Wood & Sons. Although Wood has been called the Father of British pottery, it might be more appropriate if he were called the Father of Anglo–American pottery. He has been given less recognition in his own country than other potters because he concentrated on making products for export. Besides the creamware bust of Washington (see Figure 69), probably made during Washington's lifetime, a basalt bust labeled "Washington: born 1732, died 1799" is attributed to Wood. The Wood firm also made a statuette of Washington and one of Benjamin Franklin.

26

Fig. 26 City Hotel, New York. Printed in dark blue. Made by R. S. W. (MATTATUCK MUSEUM. PHOTOGRAPH BY CHARLES KLAMKIN)

Fig. 27 Flagstaff Pavilion in the Battery, New York. Printed in dark blue. Made by R. S. W. (MATTATUCK MUSEUM. PHOTOGRAPH BY CHARLES KLAMKIN)

Fig. 28 The Battery. Printed in dark blue. Made by R. S. W. (MATTATUCK MUSEUM. PHOTOGRAPH BY CHARLES KLAMKIN)

Fig. 29 Union Line (steamboat, Troy Line). Printed in dark blue. Made by Enoch Wood & Sons. (MATTATUCK MUSEUM. PHOTOGRAPH BY CHARLES KLAMKIN)

Fig. 30 Boston State House (chaise in foreground). Printed in dark blue. Made by Rogers. (MATTATUCK MUSEUM. PHOTOGRAPH BY CHARLES KLAMKIN)

Fig. 31 Octagon Church, Boston. Printed in dark blue. Made by Ridgway. (MATTATUCK MUSEUM. PHOTOGRAPH BY CHARLES KLAMKIN)

Several border designs can be attributed to Wood's firm. The first is a border of scroll medallions with cartouches bearing inscriptions. Another typical Wood border design has a variety of seashells. A wreath of large flowers is another popular Wood border and a group of Lafayette-related plates has borders of iris, hollyhock, and grapes. A later period of printed plates, made after the firm had become Enoch Wood & Sons, carried borders of fruit and flowers. These plates were not the old dark blue, but were printed in black, brown, red, purple, light blue, and green.

The pottery firm of A. Stevenson was opened in 1808 as Bucknall & Stevenson in Cobridge, Staffordshire. Stevenson seems to have become sole owner a few years later. He hired artist W. G. Wall, who had come to New York from Dublin in 1818, to make paintings for copperplates to be used as transfers for blue and white china. Unlike Enoch Wood, Stevenson produced a great deal of printed ware for the British market as well as for export. Stevenson's most popular border was a design of flowers and scrollwork.

Stevenson's firm was taken over in 1818 by Ralph and James Clews and operated as R. & J. Clews until 1838. James Clews came to the United States in 1836 and embarked on what was to be an unsuccessful venture into potting in Troy, Indiana. Clews used a variety of borders, the most noted one being festoons containing names of the fifteen existing states. A flowered border with stars and the wingspread eagle was also used by Clews on his pottery for the American market.

A series called "Picturesque Views" was issued by Clews about 1825. The artist Wall had painted a group of Hudson River scenes, and these were published in a portfolio in 1824. The engravings on the plates were by I. Hill. These scenes, surrounded by borders of birds and flowers, were used by Clews on his pottery.

John and William Ridgway were also sons of a Staffordshire potter, and they went into their father's business around the beginning of the nineteenth century. After his death the firm became known as J. & W. Ridgway. The earliest Ridgway plant was at Hanley, Staffordshire, but shortly after the father's death the sons invested in another pottery at Shelton. It is thought that the patriotic earthenware made for the American market during this period was produced in the Shelton plant. The Ridgways produced one series of blue and white printed plates for the American market. They all have a border of rose-leaf medallions, and the center motifs include buildings in Boston, Philadelphia, and New York, as well as landmarks of other American cities and towns.

The production of "Beauties of America" plates by the Ridgways was discontinued in 1830. It was in that year that John Ridgway and his brother dissolved their partnership. John continued to carry on the business alone until his retirement in 1858. One of the best-known patterns made by John Ridgway for the American market is "Log Cabin" or "Columbian Star," which was issued for the presidential campaign of 1840. These plates were very popular and were printed in a variety of colors. Dinner sets, tea sets, and even a child's toy set were made and printed with the log cabin motif, which was supposed to represent the humble beginnings of William Henry Harrison. The price of a dinner plate was seven cents.

William Ridgway, meanwhile, turned his attention almost solely to the American market. He was an astute businessman and established agencies in the United States for the purpose of promoting and selling his goods. He came to the United States sometime after his break with the firm that was run by his brother and started plans to erect a pottery in Kentucky. Ridgway had investments in about five potteries in England, and business reverses and unfortunate investments caused him to abandon the partially erected pottery in America. It was never completed.

Fig. 32 Mitchell and Freeman's China and Glass Warehouses, Boston. Printed in dark blue. Made by Wm. Adams. (MATTATUCK MUSEUM. PHOTOGRAPH BY CHARLES KLAMKIN)

Fig. 33 Sternwheel steamboat, Philadelphia Dam and Waterworks. Printed in dark blue.
Maker unknown. (MATTATUCK MUSEUM. PHOTOGRAPH BY CHARLES KLAMKIN)

Fig. 34 Park Theater, New York. Printed in dark blue. Made by Ralph Stevenson and Williams.
(MATTATUCK MUSEUM. PHOTOGRAPH BY CHARLES KLAMKIN)

Fig. 35 Capitol at Washington with cows in foreground. Made by Enoch Wood & Sons. (MATTA-TUCK MUSEUM. PHOTOGRAPH BY CHARLES KLAMKIN)

Fig. 36 Historic elm, Pittsfield, Massachusetts, Printed in dark blue. Made by Clews. (MATTATUCK MUSEUM. PHOTOGRAPH BY CHARLES KLAMKIN)

Another potter who had a successful career manufacturing almost exclusively for the American market was Joseph Stubbs. He used an eagle, flower, and scroll border on his American printed wares. Stubbs, like many of his contemporaries, did not usually sign his plates, although, occasionally, one can be found with "Stubbs" impressed on it. However, the Stubbs' border design is unique, and all printed earthenware bearing that design is attributed to Joseph Stubbs.

The Mayer family—Thomas, John, and Joshua—took over the Dale Hall Works in Burslem from Joseph Stubbs in 1829. While there is no evidence that this firm made any printed ware for the American market, there exist today some historical plates bearing the mark of T. Mayer that are bordered with designs of trumpet flowers, stars, and wheel-shaped ornaments. Center decoration for the Mayer plates were seals or arms of the original thirteen states.

Some of the most handsome of the early blue and white plates are marked "R. S. W." or "R. S. & W." These were probably made by the firm of Ralph Stevenson and Williams of Cobridge. Two border patterns can be found on wares marked in this manner: a border of oak leaves and acorns and another of vases of flowers and scrollwork. The oak-leaf and acorn border is a favorite among collectors. Ralph Stevenson evidently was also sole proprietor of a firm that bore his name. He made dark blue printed ware and later printed the same patterns in other colors. His borders were vine-leaf designs.

The Staffordshire potter William Adams was in business alone from the beginning of the nineteenth century until about 1829, when his firm became William Adams & Sons. Dark blue plates with borders of foliage were made by the Adamses at Stoke-upon-Trent. Later, the firm produced plates in other colors with designs relating to America. These later plates, printed in pink, black, or red, have borders of roses in baskets and are marked with a cornucopia and eagle. Another Adams border has medallions containing sailors and ships. Animals and roses are the subject matter of still another issue of Adams plates printed with American views.

Spencer Rogers produced several American designs with floral borders. There are three different views of the Boston State House that are known to have been produced by Rogers. At least one design is attributed to a firm called E. & G. Phillips, about which little is known. A dark blue plate with a picture of Benjamin Franklin's tomb came from this Longport, Staffordshire, potter.

The firm of J. & J. Jackson made some rather late plates with American views printed in red, light blue, lilac, black, or brown. A floral border adorns the Jackson plates, of which there are about thirty different kinds. Thomas Godwin of Burslem Wharf was a neighbor of the Jackson firm, and he made nine or ten different plates with American views. The Godwin borders featured the convolvulus and nasturtium, and plates were printed in a variety of colors including green, brown, and light blue.

Plates marked "C. M." were made by Charles Meigh, the grandson of Job Meigh, who was also a potter of some importance. Between 1830 and 1840 the younger Meigh produced a series of plates with American views featuring a border pattern of moss and chickweed. A variety of colors was used for the engravings.

Thomas Green is the potter responsible for plates marked "T. G." These plates

Fig. 37 Erie Canal. Entrance into the Hudson at Albany. Printed in dark blue. (MATTATUCK MUSEUM. PHOTOGRAPH BY CHARLES KLAMKIN)

were produced in Fenton, England, between 1847 and 1859. All Green's plates have the same subject matter as decoration: the signing of the treaty between William Penn and the Indians. There are six different versions, however, and the engravings are more whimsical than historically accurate. The foliage is tropical, and Oriental buildings can be seen in the background. Green's borders are somewhat unusual and are made up of various diamond shapes and other geometrical patterns.

The firm of Joseph Heath & Co. made earthenware for the American market in 1829. One rather well-known center pattern used by this company is the "Residence of Richard Jordan." Richard Jordan was a Quaker preacher who died in 1826, and it is likely that the plates were ordered by his friends as a memorial. The original drawing for these plates was done by an American, W. Mason, who taught art in Philadelphia. F. Kearney did the engraving. The pattern was extremely popular in Pennsylvania and New Jersey. The plates had a floral border and were printed in a variety of colors.

Other Staffordshire potters who enjoyed a long period of trade in patriotic china with America are the J. & T. Edwards firm of Burslem; John Tams of Longton; Mellor, Venables Co. of Burslem; F. M. & Co. of Hanley; G. L. A. & Bro.; Thomas Ford & Co. of Hanley; and an unidentified potter who signed his works "C. C." The latter used a border called "Catskill Moss."

With all these potters accounted for, there are still others who were making patriotic and political china for the American market that cannot be identified. There were no laws governing the identification of imported china until 1891, when a law was passed stipulating that the country of origin had to be marked on the piece if the wares were to be sold in the United States. After this time, however, it became common practice for all British potters to sign their wares. On the old blue and white and even on the later printed china, the mark of the manufacturer is the exception rather than the rule.

6

WEDGWOOD AND THE AMERICAN MARKET

Although following the War of 1812 and the lifting of the "long embargo" Josiah Wedgwood's company continued to manufacture pottery for the American market and enjoyed a brisk trade with America throughout the nineteenth century, it is doubtful that it manufactured any of the patriotic blue and white plates in the first half of the century that brought its fellow Staffordshire potters so much business. There are several reasons for this. First, Josiah Wedgwood was dedicated to producing quality merchandise that other potters did not manufacture. The blue and white plates were, of necessity, rather poor in quality—even by early nineteenth-century standards. They were fairly heavy, and the clay used was coarse and unrefined. The plates were made to sell to customers who could not spend more than a few cents apiece for "china" plates, and in many cases the blue and white historical plates were the first china that American families owned. The more affluent and educated Americans purchased French or Chinese porcelain, and many still preferred Wedgwood's Queen's Ware.

Once the blue and white historical plates went out of fashion among the middle classes, printed plates in colors other than blue and white were made. Often plates were printed in more than one color, the printing process having been refined somewhat by the middle of the century. By this time the scenes used were more often of the rolling English countryside and of English castles than of American sites.

Although Josiah Wedgwood was the first British potter to realize the great potential in American trade, it was not until 1880 that his company, still run by

Fig. 38 The Old South Church and Trinity Church, Boston. Tiles made for Jones, McDuffie &
Stratton Co. by Wedgwood ca. 1890. Printed in black. (MR. AND MRS. ALEXANDER SCHAFFER.
PHOTOGRAPH BY CHARLES KLAMKIN)

Fig. 39 Boston Tea Party. Plate
made for Jones, McDuffie &
Stratton Co. by Wedgwood ca.
1900. Printed in medium blue.
(MR. AND MRS. ALEXANDER
SCHAFFER. PHOTOGRAPH BY
CHARLES KLAMKIN)

his descendents, opened a branch of the business that was unique in the British pottery industry. Josiah Wedgwood and Sons, under the proprietorship of Godfrey, Clement Francis, and Lawrence Wedgwood, began to manufacture commemorative ware exclusively for the American market. This branch of the company continues to be successful to this day.

Since 1880 tiles, plates, portrait medallions, busts, and hundreds of other ceramic objects have been made by Wedgwood that are never even seen by its British customers. Many of these objects commemorate special American events, people, and places or anniversaries of a patriotic or political nature, and some represent organizations and educational institutions. These items are usually produced in limited quantities and frequently are made to order. A great many of them are never offered to the public through Wedgwood's usual channels but are sold or given away through the organization, city, school, or committee that ordered them. Certain national events, however, such as the restoration of a historical site or an anniversary such as the American bicentennial, are the cause for designs and issues that are nationally advertised and sold in stores.

Many of the nineteenth-century commemorative objects by Wedgwood bear the stamp of Jones, McDuffie & Stratton Co. of Boston or Wm. Plummer & Co.

Fig. 40 Bunker Hill Monument. Plate made for Jones, McDuffie & Stratton Co. by Wedgwood. Printed in medium blue. (MR. AND MRS. ALEXANDER SCHAFFER. PHOTOGRAPH BY CHARLES KLAMKIN)

Fig. 41 Battle on Lexington Common. Plate made for Jones, McDuffie & Stratton Co. by Wedgwood ca. 1900. (MR. AND MRS. ALEXANDER SCHAFFER. PHOTOGRAPH BY CHARLES KLAMKIN)

of New York. These two stores were the major importers and distributors of wares from the Wedgwood firm in the latter part of the nineteenth century and the early part of this century.

Around 1880 the Wedgwood company began the manufacture of a series of printed historical and patriotic plates for the American market that used as motifs mainly historic sites from in and around Boston. These plates were meant to appeal to a segment of the American population that had already realized the value of the older blue and white plates and were beginning to collect them and write about them. The Wedgwood plates were sold through Jones, McDuffie & Stratton Co. for fifty cents apiece and were widely advertised. New engravings were sent to Wedgwood of such places as "Longfellow's House (1843)," "Town House, Boston (1657–1711)," or "Park St. Church, Boston." Besides Massachusetts' historical sites and landmarks, scenes from other areas of the United States were used. These were all modern views, however, and no attempt was made to reproduce the earlier blue and white plates of other artists and manufacturers. For the first time, areas outside of New England, Philadelphia, and New York were recorded on plates. Wedgwood, by 1900, had also made plates for the "Lincoln, Nebraska, State Capitol," the "Antlers at Colorado Springs, Col.," and

Fig. 42 Boston in 1768. Plate made for Jones, McDuffie & Stratton Co. by Wedgwood ca. 1900. (MR. AND MRS. ALEXANDER SCHAFFER. PHOTOGRAPH BY CHARLES KLAMKIN)

Fig. 43 Souvenir plates were ordered in 1901 for special customers in California by Jones, McDuffie & Stratton Co. Carmel Mission, San Fernando Rey Mission, San Gabriel Archangel Mission, and San Luis Rey De Francia Mission were all subjects for these plates. Marked "Wedgwood, Etruria, England." (MR. AND MRS. ALEXANDER SCHAFFER. PHOTOGRAPH BY CHARLES KLAMKIN)

the "Santa Barbara Mission, Los Angeles, Cal." Two souvenir plates were also made for St. Augustine, Florida. These plates were immediately popular and have since become collector's items (see Appendix).

In the first thirty years of this century the Wedgwood firm would oblige anyone who wanted his house or any other design printed on a limited quantity of dinner plates made of Queen's Ware or pearlware. These plates were printed in mulberry or blue and were often given to members of a large family as favors at parties or to remind them of the "old homestead." This was not a very expensive indulgence, since the plates were sold at a cost of a quarter apiece to the customer.

Since 1919, when a branch called Josiah Wedgwood & Sons, Inc. was estab-

Fig. 44 A popular blue printed plate made by Wedgwood is this view of Yale College taken from a print by A. J. Davis made in 1832.
(AUTHOR'S COLLECTION. PHOTOGRAPH BY CHARLES KLAMKIN)

Fig. 45 Mark from reverse of Yale plate showing colophon of Yale Fence.

lished in New York, the American commemorative portion of Wedgwood's business has grown to such large proportions that the manufacture of commemorative ware for the American market now includes over one hundred new designs that are introduced each year. This ware includes not only Queen's Ware plates, but jasper and basalt items as well. As America celebrates its bicentennial anniversary, the number of American pottery and porcelain commemoratives will increase, and in honor of the occasion several special series have already been announced by Josiah Wedgwood and Sons Limited.

The issuing of new commemoratives to be sold nationally has also drawn attention to those objects Wedgwood made in the past for the American market, and these are now eagerly sought by collectors. One of these is the Garfield memorial pitcher (see Plate 12). For a long while the many Wedgwood collectors in this country were not overly excited about Wedgwood ceramics that were made exclusively for this market, but these historical items have of late taken on new importance.

The motifs used by Wedgwood to decorate the American patriotic pottery and porcelain that the firm has made since the end of the last century are enormously varied. All types of ware have been made as well. Although the majority of the commemorative pieces are Queen's Ware plates and pitchers, jasperware, basalt, pearlware, caneware, drabware, and bone china have all been decorated exclu-

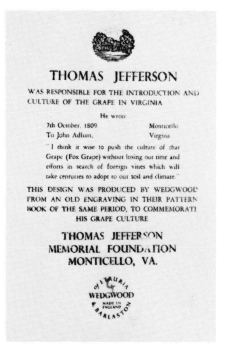

*Fig. 46 Specially designed plate for the Thomas Jefferson Memorial
Foundation, Monticello, Virginia. Made by Wedgwood.* (PRIVATE
COLLECTION. PHOTOGRAPH BY CHARLES KLAMKIN)

*Fig. 47 Mark on reverse of Thomas
Jefferson plate.*

*Fig. 49 Mark on pitcher at left showing store
for which pitcher was made.*

*Fig. 48 Printed and hand-enameled pitcher made for
Rhode Island tricentennial in 1936 with figure of founder,
Roger Williams, and quotation.* (AUTHOR'S COLLECTION.
PHOTOGRAPH BY CHARLES KLAMKIN)

Fig. 50 *Washington bowl. Modern. Designed for Wedgwood by Alan Price.*
(PHOTOGRAPH BY ROBERT E. HURWITZ)

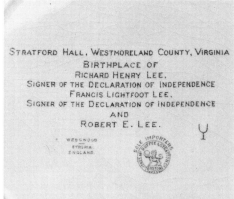

Fig. 51 Above *Mark of Lee Homestead plate explaining significance of print.*

Fig. 52 Left *Lee Homestead in Virginia. Plate with embossed border has printed decoration in red in center. Made by Wedgwood.* (AUTHOR'S COLLECTION. PHOTOGRAPH BY CHARLES KLAMKIN)

sively for the American market. Many of the eighteenth-century portrait medallions made of American patriots such as Washington, Franklin, and Jefferson have been reproduced. In some cases, modern artists have designed new versions of the portrait medallion.

New issues of plate series with historical motifs are put out with a certain amount of frequency. "American Sailing Ships" is an example of one series that, although not very old, has already become desirable for collectors (see Figures 114-115). It is common practice for American stores that ordinarily carry Wedgwood products to have special bowls, plates, or plaques with decoration of patriotic or local interest made exclusively for them. When the amount ordered is sufficient, Wedgwood will design and manufacture an item and market it exclusively in that one store. Such a case is the "Federal Bowl" designed by Alan Price and made by Wedgwood in limited quantity for Martin's Store in Washington, D. C.

Another example of a special issue is "The First Americans" series of basalt portraits of twelve American Indians in bas-relief on plaques that is currently being produced for James and James, a store in Miami, Oklahoma. Although nationally advertised, each portrait is being made in a limited quantity of 500. The original drawings for the portraits are being made by Charles Banks Wilson, and the modeling for the portraits is being done by Eric Owen. The first plaque to be released in this series is a portrait of Chief Black Hawk of the Sauk and the Fox tribes. The plaques are eight inches in diameter, and each plaque will be individually numbered and back-stamped in gold. Other notable American Indians to be commemorated in this series, to be issued one a year, are Sequoyah (Cherokee), Chief Joseph (Nez-Perce), Pontiac (Ottawa), Tecumseh (Shawnee), Powhowtan (Powhowtan), Osceola (Seminole), Red Cloud (Sioux), Pushmataha (Choktaw), Red Jacket (Seneca), Geronimo (Apache), and Sacajawea, the only woman, of the Shoshoni tribe.

Wedgwood's first special issue in honor of the American bicentennial is a series of sweet dishes. Thirteen compotiers are being produced with the last of the series to be made in 1976. The first of this series is a boxed set of two matching blue and white jasper sweet dishes, the first bearing the state seal of Virginia and the other a portrait of Thomas Jefferson. These editions will be limited only to the degree that each will be produced until the next in the series is issued.

A series of four basalt busts of American presidents has been issued recently. The four presidents so honored are Washington, Lincoln, Kennedy, and Eisenhower. The modeler was Donald Brindley. These collector's items were issued in limited editions of 2,000 each, and included with each bust was a short biography of the president represented. Modern jasper sweet dishes for collectors have also been made with portraits of Presidents Kennedy, Truman, Eisenhower, and Nixon in white bas-relief. Somehow, it appears that President Johnson was overlooked by the Wedgwood firm as a suitable subject for a bas-relief portrait.

In 1881, the Wedgwood firm, having just ventured into the business of manufacturing tiles, made small calendar tiles that were advertising items both for Wedgwood and for Jones, McDuffie & Stratton Co. of Boston. One side of the tile had a printed calendar for the year in which it was made, and the reverse side had an engraving of a landmark Boston building or historical scene. These tiles were made until 1929, and historical sites other than those in Boston were also used as subject matter. The tile for 1906 has an engraving of the Jones, McDuffie & Stratton Co. store on Franklin Street in Boston. Calendar tiles were printed in black, sepia, or, in rare cases, polychrome. They were either given away to preferred customers of the store or sold for a few cents (see Figures 53, 54).

Fig. 53 Creamware calendar tile, printed in black, made for Jones, McDuffie & Stratton Co. On reverse side is calendar for year 1912. (JO-ANNE BLUM, INC. PHOTOGRAPH BY CHARLES KLAMKIN)

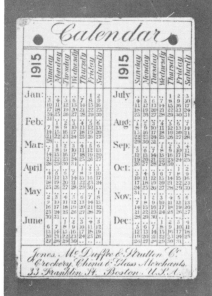

Figure. 54 Calendar tile, printed on creamware in black. Cunard Line Dock, (New) Boston.
Reverse is calendar for 1915. (JO-ANNE BLUM, INC. PHOTOGRAPH BY CHARLES KLAMKIN)

Modern Wedgwood commemoratives are often designs by the current Wedgwood American artist-in-residence, Alan Price. He designed a Washington presidential bowl in creamware to special order for American Heritage, which had the bowl produced in a limited edition for its book-club members. The original bowl from which the Price designs were adapted is owned by the Metropolitan Museum of Art in New York. It is of the Liverpool type and dates back to the eighteenth century. Price has also designed the engravings for a popular series of patriotic plates, the "Federal City" series, which was produced by Wedgwood for Charles Schwartz in Washington, D. C. "Nineteenth-century Atlanta Views" by Alan Price were commissioned by Rich's Store in that city for its centennial in 1967, and a group of plates with Chicago views was commissioned in 1968 for the Illinois centennial.

Another commemorative issued for American Heritage as a premium to promote its book *The Rise of the Republic* is a platter showing the battle between the H.M.S. *Java* and the U.S.S. *Constitution* on December 29, 1812. The original drawing for this platter was done in 1938 by an American artist, George C. Wales.

In 1930 a series of commemorative plates was designed by American artists and made by Wedgwood for Jones, McDuffie & Stratton Co. A catalog advertising

48

Fig. 55 St. Clement Danes Church. Plate, creamware, Edmé shape. Made by Wedgwood during World War II to raise money for British war relief. Sponsored by the British War Relief Society, United States. (MR. AND MRS. JOHN A. COE. PHOTOGRAPH BY CHARLES KLAMKIN)

Fig. 56 Mark on reverse of plate for British war relief.

the first edition of these plates was issued by the store. Prophetically, the claim was made in the introduction that

It is certain that just as the early Liverpool ware now brings high prices in the auction rooms, these commemorative plates will also increase in value as time goes on. The first edition plates, especially, carrying private identification marks, will eventually take their place with those things of beauty which may be classed as rare.

Included in this series were Harvard plates designed by Professor Kenneth John Conant of the fine arts department of that school. Professor Conant designed twelve views of the Harvard campus as it looked in 1930. The plates are earthenware printed in blue.

There are, of course, hundreds of other pieces of pottery of a patriotic or political nature that have been designed by Wedgwood for the American market and manufactured throughout this century. The establishment in 1919 of an American corporation by Wedgwood helped to increase this kind of production by the parent firm in Great Britain, and presently it is safe to say that most American commemorative china is made by Wedgwood.

There have been special issues made during this century for the American market that are of particular interest to historians and collectors. The first was

Fig. 57 View of the Supreme Court. Part of the "Federal City" series designed by Alan Price for Wedgwood. Produced for Charles Schwartz, Washington, D.C. (PHOTOGRAPH COURTESY OF JOSIAH WEDGWOOD AND SONS LIMITED)

Fig. 58 Reproduction of creamware bowl made for the Metropolitan Museum of Art.
(PHOTOGRAPH COURTESY OF JOSIAH WEDGWOOD AND SONS LIMITED)

made during World War I, when the Wedgwood firm had temporarily abandoned much of its regular production in order to produce war materials. Prior to America's entry into the war, an American Anglophile, Mrs. Robert Coleman Taylor of New York, designed a china pattern to be made in Wedgwood Queen's Ware and bone china. This ware was ordered through Wm. Plummer & Co. of New York, although it was never sold in that store. The design consisted of the American shield surrounded by the flags of the Allies. Mrs. Coleman's plan was to sell tea sets "from tea table to tea table" to raise money for "war sufferers." She believed that "In all collections of old china there are treasured pieces made to perpetuate important historical events" (see Plate 21).

"Liberty China" was Mrs. Coleman's way of commemorating World War I and America's part in it. Through her industry in enlisting Plummer's and Wedgwood's help in producing and importing this china, 4,983 pieces of bone china and 4,266 pieces of Queen's Ware with the colorful Liberty pattern were made. All this, with the exception of two tea services and two bowls made for British customers, was shipped to America throughout the war, and miraculously, none of it was lost at sea. As soon as the war was over and the last piece had been shipped, the copperplates were destroyed according to an agreement between Wedgwood and Mrs. Coleman, so that no more could ever be produced. Considering that the china was never advertised and never sold

50

THE EMPIRE STATE BUILDING
New York City

The world's tallest building soars majestically skyward - its 102 story elegance rising high above busy New York streets on the site of the original Waldorf Astoria Hotel. Heads of State, Dignitaries, and millions of people from all over the world marvel at the five-state view from its Observatories. Transmission center for all New York television stations, the Empire State Building is truly "The Eighth Wonder of the World."

Fig. 59 Engraving of the Empire State Building printed on creamware in black. Made by Wedgwood on Edmé shape. (MR. AND MRS. ALEXANDER SCHAFFER. PHOTOGRAPH BY CHARLES KLAMKIN)

Fig. 60 Marks and description of Empire State Building on reverse of commemorative plate.

Fig. 61 Plate commemorating 350th anniversary of the sailing of the Pilgrims to America. Decoration printed in tones of brown. Plate is Wedgwood's Queen's Ware. (PHOTOGRAPH COURTESY OF JOSIAH WEDGWOOD AND SONS LIMITED)

51

through a retail outlet, it is amazing that the china was purchased by people in thirty-eight states, Hawaii, and the District of Columbia as well as in ten foreign countries.

Of all the Liberty china that was made only two dozen cups and saucers were lost—between New York and Baltimore in September 1917. A tea set of Queen's Ware with cups and saucers and plates never found its way to its destination in Chestnut Hill, Pennsylvania. Mrs. Coleman also recorded that "a complete afternoon tea-set sent as a gift to the Prince of Wales when he was in New York was in some way mislaid, and . . . had never been received."

In bone china, cups and saucers, plates in five-, six-, seven-, eight- and nine-inch sizes were made, as well as tea pots, sugar bowls, cream jugs, and hot water jugs in two sizes. In Queen's Ware, cups and saucers, five-, six-, and seven-inch plates, tea pots, sugar bowls, cream jugs, and hot water jugs in two sizes were made. This wartime occupation of Mrs. Taylor's must certainly be unique in the annals of ceramics manufacture and retailing.

Even with such carefully documented items as Liberty china, there is a special category for the knowledgeable collector. Since Liberty china was only ordered through Plummer's, then Wedgwood's New York agent, but was never sold

Fig. 62 Blue and white jasper sweet dish commemorating 350th anniversary of sailing of Pilgrims, made by Wedgwood in 1970. (PHOTO-GRAPH COURTESY OF JOSIAH WEDGWOOD AND SONS LIMITED)

through the store, Mrs. Taylor was extremely upset by an oversight at the Wedgwood firm. The first shipment of 500 bone china cups and saucers; 100 seven-inch plates; 15 teapots, sugar bowls, and cream jugs; 500 Queen's Ware cups and saucers; and 250 seven-inch plates in that ware arrived with the name of "Wm. H. Plummer & Co." stamped in red beneath the Wedgwood imprint. Mrs. Coleman, upset by this error, wrote later, "This was never repeated." The most desirable of all Liberty china is, of course, that which is imprinted with the Plummer name.

Another related item for Wedgwood commemorative collectors is the small booklet Mrs. Coleman wrote in 1924 giving a full accounting of the money received from the sale of Liberty china. This booklet was issued in a limited edition of 1,000 and was privately distributed.

During World War II Josiah Wedgwood & Sons, Inc., produced a series of commemorative plates called "Old London Scenes" to raise money for British war relief. This series, although it bore British scenes, was made to be sold in the United States before it entered the war. The plates were hand-engraved in sepia on the Edme shape and sold for twenty-four dollars with four dollars of this amount being donated to British war relief.

7

AMERICAN POTTERS AND PATRIOTIC CHINA

Historically, British potters have understood the American market far better than have American ceramics producers. If Josiah Wedgwood feared that competition from American potters would eventually preclude further extensive trade with customers on this continent, he needn't have. Many small potteries were started on American soil at the end of the eighteenth and the first half of the nineteenth century, but few of them survived for any length of time. Certainly, no truly innovative work was produced in America until the last quarter of the nineteenth century.

The early history of American pottery is closely tied in both a negative and positive way with the British pottery industry. There were some successful attempts by Americans to pirate skilled help from England, and there is some evidence that, in retribution, British potters paid workers in this country to sabotage any efforts to make comparable pottery here. Claims were made in late eighteenth-century newspaper advertisements by potters in Philadelphia and Boston that their pottery was "equal to any imported from England."

"Tortoise-shell, Cream and Green colour Plates, Dishes, Coffee and Tea Pots, Cups and Saucers, and all other Articles in the Potter's Business" were advertised as being produced "at the new Factory in New Boston" in 1769. The potters in Philadelphia, New York, and Boston also advertised for samples of clay and for apprentices to learn the pottery trade. Little is known about the early attempts in this country to produce American pottery. However, a few of the Staffordshire potters who had been trading successfully with America left their own country to start in the industry here. Such a potter was James Clews, who had manu-

factured many of the blue and white historical plates for this market. He closed
his factory in England and came to America in 1829, settling in Troy, Indiana.
Clews had thought that the clay at Troy, on the Ohio River, would be suitable
for use in the same type of ware he had made in England, but it turned out that
it was impossible to make whiteware from the available clay, so eventually
Clews returned to England. The Indiana Pottery Company, which Clews founded,
made yellow and Rockingham wares under the supervision of a variety of
potters until it burned down in 1854. However, the blue and white printed
ware that Clews had made in England was never produced in his American
factory.

*Fig. 63 Seated figure of Liberty holding the American
flag. Parian porcelain with blue slip decoration. Made
at Bennington, Vermont.* (MATTATUCK MUSEUM.
PHOTOGRAPH BY CHARLES KLAMKIN)

*Fig. 64 Posy holder made at Bennington. American
eagle of Parian porcelain holding Belleek flower.
Turquoise enamel and gilding.* (MATTATUCK MUSEUM.
PHOTOGRAPH BY CHARLES KLAMKIN)

Fig. 65 General Stark toby pitcher, flint enamel. Made at
Bennington. (Height: 6 in.) (MATTATUCK MUSEUM. PHOTOGRAPH
BY CHARLES KLAMKIN)

Fig. 66 Clay pipe made for Henry Clay.
(SMITHSONIAN INSTITUTION PHOTOGRAPH)

Another member of a famous Staffordshire pottery family who tried his luck
in America was William Ridgway. He started building a large pottery in Kentucky, but the buildings were never completed and the idea was apparently
abandoned.

Perhaps one of the few successful British potters who worked in this country
in the nineteenth century was Daniel Greatbach, who came from a family of
noted English potters. One of the reasons for his success is probably that he
did not go into his own business but found work as a modeler, first for the
American Pottery Manufacturing Company in Jersey City and, later, for the
United States Pottery in Bennington, Vermont. Greatbach is probably responsible
for the Vermont firm's many years of success in the pottery industry.

In 1846 Christopher Weber Fenton, Henry D. Hall, and Julius Norton, all of
Bennington, Vermont, opened a pottery for the purpose of making yellow (cream),
white, and Rockingham wares. They brought John Harrison from England to do
the modeling for them. Harrison did not stay long, but the company remained
in business and expanded. In 1849 it became the United States Pottery. A

PLATE 1

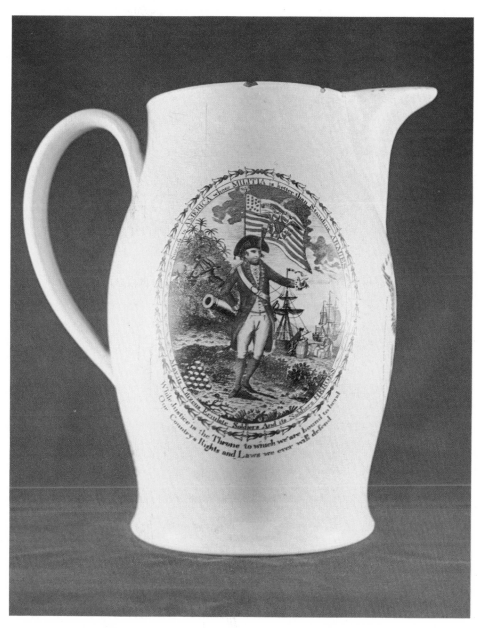

Liverpool jug, black print enameled in red and blue. Subject: Washington standing next to a cannon with flag and ships in background. (MATTATUCK MUSEUM. PHOTOGRAPH BY CHARLES KLAMKIN)

PLATE 2

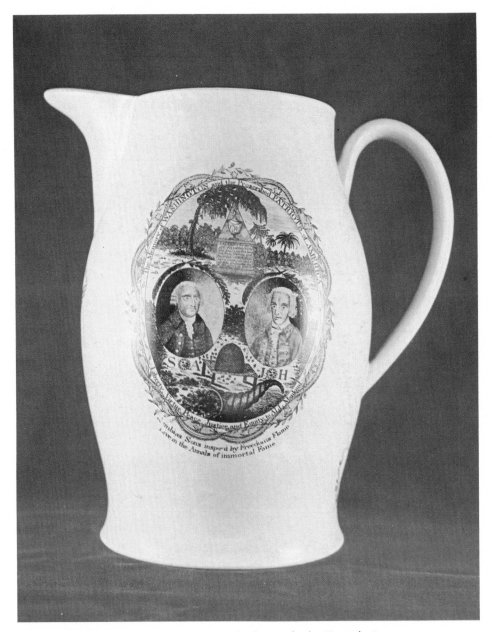

Enameled Liverpool jug with portraits of Samuel Adams and John Hancock. (MATTATUCK
MUSEUM. PHOTOGRAPH BY CHARLES KLAMKIN)

PLATE 3

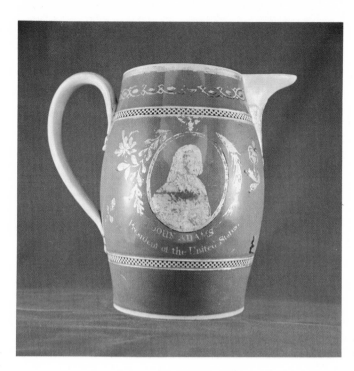

Left. *Rare Liverpool John Adams jug. Blue enamel over print, originally gilded but now worn. Black and white checked borders, top and bottom.* (MATTATUCK MUSEUM. PHOTOGRAPH BY CHARLES KLAMKIN)

Right. *Reverse of John Adams creamware jug with ship* Orono. (MATTATUCK MUSEUM. PHOTOGRAPH BY CHARLES KLAMKIN)

PLATE 4

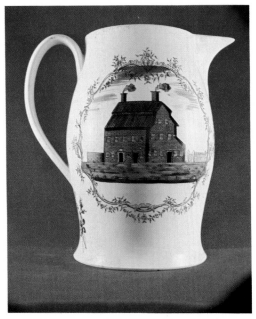

Above. *Thomas Jefferson Liverpool printed jug. Green and yellow enameling over printed wreath around portrait.* (MATTATUCK MUSEUM. PHOTOGRAPH BY CHARLES KLAMKIN)

Above. *Liverpool pitcher showing painting of first bakery in America.* (MATTATUCK MUSEUM. PHOTOGRAPH BY CHARLES KLAMKIN)

Above. *"Gallant Defense of Stonington" pitcher is printed in black and gilded. Made by Herculaneum Pottery in Liverpool.* (MATTATUCK MUSEUM. PHOTOGRAPH BY CHARLES KLAMKIN)

Above. *Reverse of Stonington pitcher has colorful print with enameling of ship flying American flag against the wind.* (MATTATUCK MUSEUM. PHOTOGRAPH BY CHARLES KLAMKIN)

PLATE 5

Above. *The states and a poem to Liberty adorn this jug printed and hand-enameled in yellow and green.* (MATTATUCK MUSEUM. PHOTOGRAPH BY CHARLES KLAMKIN)

Above. *Liverpool jug has ship* Reward *flying American flag. Printed and enameled.* (MATTATUCK MUSEUM. PHOTOGRAPH BY CHARLES KLAMKIN)

PLATE 6

Above. *Landing of the Pilgrims. Made by Enoch Wood.* (MATTATUCK MUSEUM. PHOTOGRAPH BY CHARLES KLAMKIN)

Above. *"Commodore McDonough's Victory." Made by Enoch Wood & Sons.* (MATTATUCK MUSEUM. PHOTOGRAPH BY CHARLES KLAMKIN)

PLATE 7

Above. *States design with fishermen. Portrait of Washington in border. Made by Clews.* (MATTATUCK MUSEUM. PHOTOGRAPH BY CHARLES KLAMKIN)

Above. *Standing figure mourning at the tomb of Washington.* (MATTATUCK MUSEUM. PHOTOGRAPH BY CHARLES KLAMKIN)

Above. *"Battle of Bunker Hill." Made by R. Stevenson.* (MATTATUCK MUSEUM. PHOTOGRAPH BY CHARLES KLAMKIN)

PLATE 8

Above. *Four-portrait border with Jefferson, Clinton, Lafayette, and Washington. In bottom border is vignette of entrance of Erie Canal into the Hudson at Albany. The center
print, which has nothing to do with American motifs, is of
Faulkborn Hall in England. Made by Stevenson.* (MATTA-
TUCK MUSEUM. PHOTOGRAPH BY CHARLES KLAMKIN)

Right. *Two or more color prints were used toward the mid-
dle of the nineteenth century for patriotic plates. This
Staffordshire plate is decorated with motif of flowers,
American flag, and Liberty cap.* (MR. AND MRS. LEON
WEISSEL. PHOTOGRAPH BY CHARLES KLAMKIN)

PLATE 9

Above. *Hand-decorated cup and saucer with George and Martha Washington's monograms were probably made at Bennington, Vermont, around 1880.* (AUTHOR'S COLLECTION. PHOTOGRAPH BY CHARLES KLAMKIN)

Above. *Dated salt-glaze cup plate, incised with blue glaze over design. William Henry Harrison memento.* (DEWITT COLLECTION, UNIVERSITY OF HARTFORD. PHOTOGRAPH BY CHARLES KLAMKIN)

Above. *Copper luster pitcher with black transfer portrait of Andrew Jackson.* (SMITHSONIAN INSTITUTION PHOTOGRAPH)

PLATE 10

Above. *"Harrison and Reform." Teapot with portrait of William Harrison.* (DEWITT COLLECTION, UNIVERSITY OF HARTFORD. PHOTOGRAPH BY CHARLES KLAMKIN)

Above. *Antislavery plate with motif printed from Wedgwood's eighteenth-century medallion. Bone china, printed and gilded.* (DEWITT COLLECTION, UNIVERSITY OF HARTFORD. PHOTOGRAPH BY CHARLES KLAMKIN)

Above. *Redware glazed jug with Lincoln's profile surrounded by laurel wreath. Probably a one-of-a-kind and made by an American potter.* (DEWITT COLLECTION, UNIVERSITY OF HARTFORD. PHOTOGRAPH BY CHARLES KLAMKIN)

PLATE 11

Above. *Polychrome portrait of Lincoln, possibly made during his lifetime.* (DEWITT COLLECTION, UNIVERSITY OF HARTFORD. PHOTOGRAPH BY CHARLES KLAMKIN)

Above. *Printed commemorative plate of Lincoln's tomb in Springfield, Illinois.* (DEWITT COLLECTION, UNIVERSITY OF HARTFORD. PHOTOGRAPH BY CHARLES KLAMKIN)

Above. *Portraits of first ladies are not often used for plate decoration. This Mary Lincoln plate is one of a series made in Japan around the beginning of this century.* (DEWITT COLLECTION, UNIVERSITY OF HARTFORD. PHOTOGRAPH BY CHARLES KLAMKIN)

Above. *Two-color printed plate commemorating Lincoln and his house in Springfield, Illinois. Made by Petrus Regout & Co., Maastricht, Holland.* (DEWITT COLLECTION, UNIVERSITY OF HARTFORD. PHOTOGRAPH BY CHARLES KLAMKIN)

PLATE 12

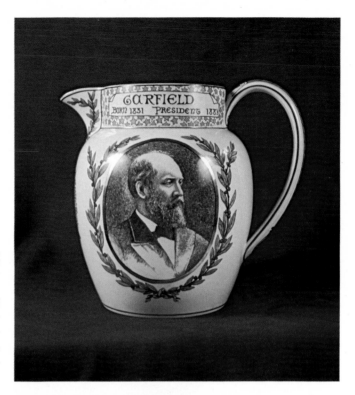

Right. *Front of Garfield memorial pitcher, cream-ware, printed and hand-painted. Made and marked by Wedgwood.* (DEWITT COLLECTION, UNIVERSITY OF HARTFORD. PHOTO-RAPH BY CHARLES KLAM-KIN)

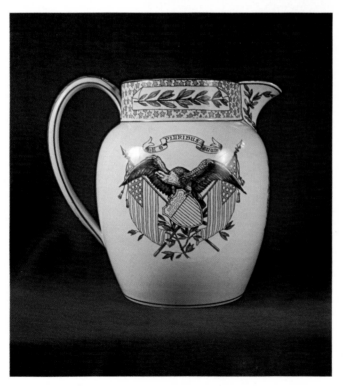

Left. *Reverse of Garfield pitcher, showing crossed flags, shield, and eagle.* (DEWITT COLLECTION, UNIVERSITY OF HARTFORD. PHOTOGRAPH BY CHARLES KLAMKIN)

PLATE 13

Above. *Plate with print of James Garfield.* (DEWITT
COLLECTION, UNIVERSITY OF HARTFORD. PHOTOGRAPH BY
CHARLES KLAMKIN)

Above. *One could manipulate this
campaign toy scale with bisque dolls of
Grover Cleveland and Benjamin Harrison
to decide who was the heavier candidate.
For all Cleveland's girth, Harrison won.*
(DEWITT COLLECTION, UNIVERSITY OF
HARTFORD. PHOTOGRAPH BY CHARLES
KLAMKIN)

Above. *Pink glazed pitcher had portrait of
Benjamin Harrison on one side.* (SMITHSONIAN
INSTITUTION PHOTOGRAPH)

Above. *Levi Parsons Morton, Harrison's running
mate, is portrayed on reverse of Harrison pitcher.*
(SMITHSONIAN INSTITUTION PHOTOGRAPH)

PLATE 14

Above. *McKinley and Theodore Roosevelt on plate issued for campaign in 1900.* (DEWITT COLLECTION, UNIVERSITY OF HARTFORD. PHOTOGRAPH BY CHARLES KLAMKIN)

Left. *Plate with portrait of McKinley, made during his administration.* (DEWITT COLLECTION, UNIVERSITY OF HARTFORD. PHOTOGRAPH BY CHARLES KLAMKIN)

PLATE 15

Above. *The same transfer print in color of William McKinley can be found on many different types of pottery and porcelain, most of it imported either from Germany or France. This plate, however, was made by Knowles, Taylor and Knowles, East Liverpool, Ohio.* (DEWITT COLLECTION, UNIVERSITY OF HARTFORD. PHOTOGRAPH BY CHARLES KLAMKIN)

Above. *This McKinley plate with carnations on the border is marked "Sèvres."* (DEWITT COLLECTION OF HARTFORD. PHOTOGRAPH BY CHARLES KLAMKIN)

Right. *Scalloped candy dish with McKinley's portrait has no mark, but was probably made in Germany.* (DEWITT COLLECTION, UNIVERSITY OF HARTFORD. PHOTOGRAPH BY CHARLES KLAMKIN)

PLATE 16

Above. *McKinley toby pitcher is one of the scarcer items from McKinley campaign. Hand-enameled.* (DEWITT COLLECTION, UNIVERSITY OF HARTFORD. PHOTOGRAPH BY CHARLES KLAMKIN)

Above. *McKinley pitcher, white porcelain with gilded rim and handle.* (DEWITT COLLECTION, UNIVERSITY OF HARTFORD. PHOTOGRAPH BY CHARLES KLAMKIN)

Above. *McKinley toby made of different clay and glazed green.* (DEWITT COLLECTION, UNIVERSITY OF HARTFORD. PHOTOGRAPH BY CHARLES KLAMKIN)

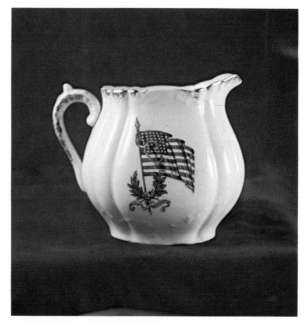

Above. *American flag is printed on reverse of McKinley pitcher.* (DEWITT COLLECTION, UNIVERSITY OF HARTFORD. PHOTOGRAPH BY CHARLES KLAMKIN)

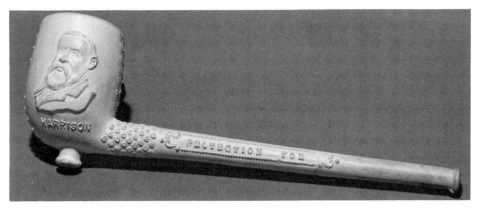

Fig. 67 Clay campaign pipe made for Benjamin Harrison. (SMITHSONIAN INSTITUTION PHOTOGRAPH)

patent for "flint enameled ware" was taken out that same year, and Daniel Greatbach was brought from New Jersey as chief modeler for the firm. Decorators were hired from abroad.

The flint enameled ware comprised only a small portion of the pottery produced at Bennington. Redware (glazed and unglazed), stoneware, scroddledware (a mixture of wedged clays of various colors made to resemble stone), mortarware, and Parian porcelain in several colors as well as white were manufactured by the United States Pottery. Many of the shapes used were made directly from British molds or adapted from British pottery types. Highly popular was a cheap imitation of Wedgwood's jasperware, in which the Bennington potters used a Parian body with colored slip in the mold. The raised decoration was not applied separately, as it was in Wedgwood jasper bas-relief, but was molded into the piece. Compared with British jasperware, the Bennington Parian was crude and primitive, but it was infinitely cheaper than the imported jasper and found a ready market in this country.

The earliest products from Bennington decorated with American motifs are stoneware jugs, pitchers, and crocks with applied or painted eagles. There are also Parian pitchers with corn husk patterns embossed on their surfaces. Various eagle forms were made from 1850 to 1858, and these were adapted to paperweights and small vases in Parian, graniteware, or Belleek porcelain (see Figure 64).

Perhaps the most charming of all the Bennington pieces that were made to appeal to patriotic Americans are the flint-glazed toby pitchers that are portraits of Benjamin Franklin, Zachary Taylor, and General Stark. The rarity of these pieces today would lead one to believe that by the second half of the nineteenth century pottery made with patriotic motifs or shaped to resemble American

Fig. 68 Pipe head for campaign of William McKinley. (MR. AND MRS. LEON WEISSEL. PHOTOGRAPH BY CHARLES KLAMKIN)

patriots had gone out of fashion. And indeed, considering the great output of the Bennington firm throughout the second half of the nineteenth century, proportionately little was decorated or shaped in this manner. Overdecorated Victorian ware comprised the bulk of the late Bennington production.

While the American potters left the production of tableware to the British, French, and Chinese potters, other types of ceramic objects were manufactured in this country very early. The American Shakers at Mount Lebanon, New York, made clay tobacco pipes from the time of their settlement in 1776. In 1690 white clay tobacco pipes were being manufactured in Philadelphia. These were long-stemmed white clay pipes that had been used in England and Holland for over a century. The American Indians, however, had made and used clay pipes hundreds of years before this time.

Pipe bowls were made after the eighteenth century in this country. It was only a short step from making plain pipe bowls to using molds to form the soft clay into head shapes or to decorate it with patriotic and political motifs. Because clay pipes are among the cheapest ceramic objects one can make and because they are given and received in an atmosphere of relaxation and good will, pipe bowls formed into small sculptures of political candidates became a rather common giveaway item during political campaigns. Clay pipes break easily and frequently are used several times and then thrown away, so there are not many campaign pipes still in existence. Some of the finest pipe heads were made by a French immigrant in New York City around 1900. A. Peyrau was only in the pipe modeling business for six or seven years, but his models of prominent Americans are highly prized by collectors. The features of his models were caricatures, and Peyrau used a light red unglazed terra cotta for his pipe bowls.

Short-stemmed white clay pipes were made for the presidential campaigns of 1888 and 1892, and both Harrison and Cleveland were modeled for this purpose by Charles Kurth of Brooklyn, New York (see Figures 66, 67, 68).

8

DESIGNS RELATING TO WASHINGTON

There is no reason why eighteenth-century British potters or the artists who engraved the designs that were used to decorate their wares should have had any true idea of what George Washington looked like until he had become president. However, this did not deter artists from drawing his likeness from any available source and adapting it to any clay body on which they were working. A few of the likenesses were totally imaginary. Josiah Wedgwood made intaglios, cameos of basalt, and portrait medallions of the profile of Washington. The artistic source for this earliest portrait was a bronze medal designed by Voltaire in 1777. The medal was inscribed "Ge. Washington, General of the Continental Army in America." The likeness was purely imaginary, and Washington is garbed in a toga because it was customary at the time to picture all contemporary heroes as Romans (see Figure 70).

Although Charles Willson Peale painted a portrait of Washington in his Virginia militia colonel's uniform as early as 1772, there is no indication that either Voltaire or Wedgwood ever saw it, nor is there any similarity between the Voltaire-designed medallion and any later portraits of Washington. In his later years, Washington was drawn, painted, and sculpted by many of the well-known artists of his time. The Staffordshire and Liverpool engravers adapted some of these artists' impressions of Washington in their designs for pitchers, plates, and mugs, both before and after Washington's death. During Wedgwood's lifetime, however, there are some other known examples of pottery or porcelain likenesses of Washington, one of them the rather primitive cream-ware bust by Enoch Wood that has already been mentioned. Another early portrait, depicting Washington in regimentals and with a queue, appears on a creamware pint mug (see Figure 71). A Wedgwood portrait bust in black basalt of Washington seems to have been made after the first president's lifetime.

The majority of portraits of George Washington to be found on pitchers, mugs, and plates, and those in busts and bas-relief are memorials and commemoratives of the first president. They were made for centennials of his birth and death and for other notable anniversaries. Such pieces have been eagerly sought and collected by Washington buffs since they were first produced. However, perhaps the most desirable of these items are the Liverpool jugs that show sentimental engravings of Washington and extol his virtues. "He in Glory, America in Tears" is the lament most often found on such jugs, and the sentiment usually accompanies Washington's likeness leaning on his own tomb. The sentimental "A Man without Example, A Patriot without Reproach" or "Died Universally Regretted" are frequently used on these "Apotheosis" jugs as well.

British potters were not without a certain amount of assurance that their wares

Fig. 69 Enoch Wood's creamware bust of Washington was made during first president's lifetime. (SMITHSONIAN INSTITUTION. PHOTOGRAPH BY CHARLES KLAMKIN)

Fig. 70 Wedgwood's earliest portrait medallion of George Washington. White bas-relief on blue jasper ground. (AUTHOR'S COLLECTION. PHOTOGRAPH BY CHARLES KLAMKIN)

Fig. 71 One of earliest examples of transfer-printed mug, made during presidency of George Washington. Printed in sepia. Original engraving by F. Morris, who signed the copperplate under portrait. (MATTATUCK MUSEUM. PHOTOGRAPH BY CHARLES KLAMKIN)

Fig. 72 Apotheosis print on Washington pitcher. Printed in black. (MATTATUCK MUSEUM. PHOTOGRAPH BY CHARLES KLAMKIN)

Fig. 73 Portrait of Washington surrounded by all the symbols of liberty. Printed in black. (MATTATUCK MUSEUM. PHOTOGRAPH BY CHARLES KLAMKIN)

Fig. 74 Print entitled "Washington in Glory, America in Tears," showing tomb of Washington and other symbols of the engraver's imagination. (MATTATUCK MUSEUM. PHOTOGRAPH BY CHARLES KLAMKIN)

Fig. 75 *Profile print in black of Washington. The words "He in Glory, America in Tears" surround portrait.* (MATTATUCK MUSEUM. PHOTOGRAPH BY CHARLES KLAMKIN)

Fig. 76 *"Hail Columbia happy land" was poem written to celebrate the freedom of a new nation. It adorns more than one Washington Liverpool jug.* (MATTATUCK MUSEUM. PHOTOGRAPH BY CHARLES KLAMKIN)

Fig. 77 *Print showing mourners at the tomb of Washington. Printed in black.* (MATTATUCK MUSEUM. PHOTOGRAPH BY CHARLES KLAMKIN)

Fig. 78 *British potters' and engravers' tribute to their own fallen heroes and also extolling Washington.* (MATTATUCK MUSEUM. PHOTOGRAPH BY CHARLES KLAMKIN)

Fig. 79 "A Man Without Example, A Patriot
Without Reproach" is how the engraver saw
the dead Washington. Printed in black with
black line around rim. (MATTATUCK MUSEUM.
PHOTOGRAPH BY CHARLES KLAMKIN)

Fig. 80 Reverse of black lined jug showing
urn with Washington's initials and facts about
Washington's life.

would appeal to a grieving America. On one pitcher (see Figure 11), which
includes in two medallions the portraits of Samuel Adams and John Hancock, is
a funeral urn with the monogram "G. W." An inscription around the base
reads "Sacred to the Memory of G. Washington who emancipated America from
Slavery and founded a Republic upon such just and equitable principles that
will survive in after ages." Around the border we read the phrase "The Memory
of Washington and the Proscribed Patriots of America, Liberty, Virtue, Peace,
Justice, and Equity to all Mankind," and underneath, "Columbia's Sons inspired
by Freedom's Flame, Live in the Annals of Immortal Fame." On the reverse side
of the same jug (which is only 11 1/4 inches high) is a portrait of Washington
in uniform, with his right hand upon his hip and his left hand pointing to vessels
from which hogsheads, bales of cotton, and other goods are being unloaded.
On the surrounding border we read, "Success to America whose Militia is better
than standing Armies. May its Citizens Emulate Soldiers and its Soldiers Heroes."
The engravers managed to squeeze more anti-British (or pro-American) sentiments into the surrounding border, which reads "While Justice is the Throne to

Fig. 81 Creamware bust of Washington, hand-enameled. Probably made for Washington bicentennial in 1932. (DEWITT COLLECTION, UNIVERSITY OF HARTFORD. PHOTOGRAPH BY CHARLES KLAMKIN)

Fig. 82 Plate made in France, printed with portrait of Washington taken from Gilbert Stuart painting. Shades of black and gray. Ca. 1830. (MATTATUCK MUSEUM. PHOTOGRAPH BY CHARLES KLAMKIN)

which we are bound to bend our Country's Rights and Laws we ever will defend."
The front of the jug is adorned with an American eagle with a shield on its
breast and thirteen stars between its outstretched wings. Under the eagle is
written "Peace, Commerce and honest Friendship with all Nations, Entangling
Alliance with none. Jefferson."

Another, smaller jug shows a bust of Washington in regimentals with the
usual lament, "He in Glory, America in Tears." On the reverse is the following
verse:

> Hail Columbia happy land,
> Hail ye patriotic band,
> Who late oppos'd oppressive laws,
> And now stand firm in freedom's cause,
> Rejoice for now the storm is gone,
> Columbia owns her chosen son.
> The rights of man shall be our boast,
> And Jefferson our favorite toast,
> Republicans behold your chief.
> He comes to give your fears relief,
> Now armed in virtue firm and true,
> Looks for support to Heaven and you.

Fig. 83 White smear-glazed stoneware pitcher with standing figure
of George Washington. Probably
made at Bennington. (MATTATUCK
MUSEUM. PHOTOGRAPH BY CHARLES
KLAMKIN)

Fig. 84 Printed portrait plate of George Washington (from Stuart portrait) made to celebrate bicentennial in 1932 of Washington's birth. Fondeville-England. Made by Soho Pottery, Cobridge, England. (DEWITT COLLECTION, UNIVERSITY OF HARTFORD. PHOTOGRAPH BY CHARLES KLAMKIN)

Fig. 85 "Commemorative Feast, in Honor of the one Hundredth Anniversary of Washington's Farewell to his Officers." Affair was held in 1883, and bowl was made to commemorate the occasion. (MRS. MARJORIE HARDY. PHOTOGRAPH BY CHARLES KLAMKIN)

Fig. 86 *Washington toby mug. Probably commemorative of Washington's bicentennial.* (DEWITT COLLECTION, UNIVERSITY OF HARTFORD. PHOTOGRAPH BY CHARLES KLAMKIN)

An eagle-flanked bust of Washington completes the decoration on the reverse side of the pitcher. It is obvious that freedom of speech was never an issue in the early days of Staffordshire and Liverpool, especially since it meant more trade with America.

Another Washington commemorative jug, which depicts the American eagle with drooping head and a female figure in tears as both contemplate a monument to Washington, contains the verse:

> *As he tills your rich glebe,*
> *The old peasant shall tell,*
> *While his bosom with Liberty glows,*
> *How your Warren expired,*
> *How Montgomery fell,*
> *And how Washington humbled your foes.*

By far the greatest number of Liverpool jugs were made as commemoratives to Washington. More rare are those pitchers with portraits of our other early patriots. John Adams, Benjamin Franklin, Thomas Jefferson, and John Hancock were all used as subject matter. Ships, maps of the states, eagles, and other motifs of a patriotic nature also appear on the surfaces of Liverpool ware. A portrait of Lafayette on an early pitcher commemorates his visit to America in 1824. It is only one of many pottery and porcelain commemoratives made to honor Lafayette during that year.

Although the majority of Washington memorial pottery and porcelain was made in Great Britain, there are objects that were produced elsewhere which are perhaps of more interest simply because they are scarcer. A French statuette of Washington by Badin Freres depicts him dressed in a yellow coat and blue vest. He carries a scroll marked "Patria." By his side is an American eagle crowing over a broken tablet that has on it a picture of the British lion. Another statuette of glazed pottery made by the same firm has Washington with his foot on a subdued British lion and the British flag. He carries a scroll with "Independence" written on it. It is thought that the likeness was taken from the Rembrandt Peale portrait of Washington. The well-known portrait of Washington by Gilbert Stuart was another source for European artists depicting the first president.

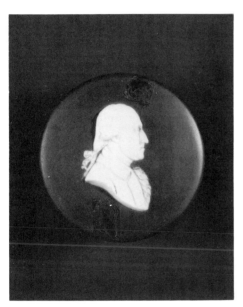

Fig. 87 Lid of Wedgwood trinket box has profile portrait of George Washington. Late nineteenth century. (MRS. MARJORIE HARDY. PHOTOGRAPH BY CHARLES KLAMKIN)

Fig. 88 Wedgwood's most recent portrait medallion of head of Washington. Blue jasper with white bas-relief. (PHOTOGRAPH COURTESY OF JOSIAH WEDGWOOD AND SONS LIMITED)

9

DESIGNS RELATING TO JOHN ADAMS, BENJAMIN FRANKLIN, AND THOMAS JEFFERSON

Compared with the volume of Washington china, there is very little in the way of china that can be associated with the presidency of John Adams. Adams did not cut the heroic figure that our first president did. Also, his appearance was less of a mystery to the British, who had never seen George Washington. Adams was the first American minister to the Court of St. James. His attempts to establish friendly relations with the British were futile, and the three years Adams spent in that country, from 1785 to 1788, were so discouraging that he asked to be called home.

Adams was elected president in 1796, in the first bipartisan election to be held in the United States. There was no provision for parties in the Constitution, and candidates were chosen by congressional caucus. Whereas there had been no opposition to the election of George Washington, the man who had served under him as vice president was opposed by Thomas Jefferson and Aaron Burr. Thomas Pinckney was on Adams' ticket. The president and vice president were elected according to the number of votes they received. Each elector voted twice, and, regardless of whether the candidate ran for the first or the second place on the ballot, the one with the most votes became president and the second highest became vice president. Thus, Thomas Jefferson became Adams' vice president. Adams himself won the election with only a three-vote majority.

The Liverpool pitcher in Plate 3 is a rare example of early Anglo-American pottery. The body of the pitcher is robin's egg blue, and it has a checkered band of black and white about two inches from the top and from the bottom. The portrait of Adams is in gilt that has become somewhat worn. The reverse side of the pitcher shows the merchant ship *Orono* under full sail. Under the portrait are the words "John Adams, President of the United States."

The relationship between John Adams and his vice president, Thomas Jefferson, grew increasingly worse during Adams's administration. They represented two different political philosophies that could not be resolved, and when Adams ran for re-election in 1800, Jefferson was nominated by the Republicans for the presidency. Jefferson was for states' rights and for discharging the national debt. He was against a standing army and in favor of free trade for all, a sentiment shared by the British pottery industry.

The Federalist party was split in the campaign, and Alexander Hamilton opposed Adams as well as Jefferson. Political name calling, now so common that

Fig. 89 Modern basalt bust of George Washington issued in limited numbers by Wedgwood. (PHOTOGRAPH COURTESY OF JOSIAH WEDGWOOD AND SONS LIMITED)

Fig. 90 Black print on Liverpool jug commemorating John Adams and made during his presidency. Transfer paper accidently was folded into the application of the print and marred Adams' portrait. (MATTATUCK MUSEUM. PHOTOGRAPH BY CHARLES KLAMKIN)

Fig. 91 Although America wasn't quite into an era of "Peace and Plenty" during John Adams' administration, British engravers and potters sent that message anyway on the reverse of Adams jug. (MATTATUCK MUSEUM. PHOTOGRAPH BY CHARLES KLAMKIN)

Fig. 92 Thomas Jefferson was the subject of a Liverpool jug made during his administration. (MATTATUCK MUSEUM. PHOTOGRAPH BY CHARLES KLAMKIN)

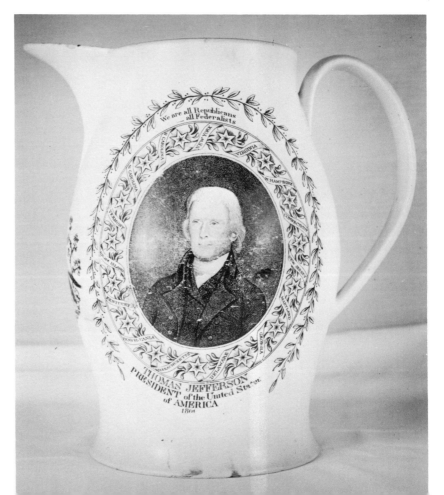

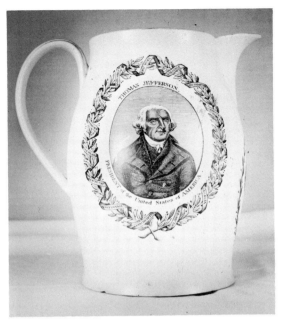

Fig. 93 This Jefferson jug, also made during the president's lifetime, is not as flattering as the previous print. (MATTATUCK MUSEUM. PHOTOGRAPH BY CHARLES KLAMKIN)

Fig. 94 This print of the reverse of Jefferson jug was used on many Liverpool jugs. (MATTATUCK MUSEUM. PHOTOGRAPH BY CHARLES KLAMKIN)

it is ignored by most voters, really began with the 1800 political campaign. Jefferson was accused of being a political fanatic, a drunkard, and the father of many illegitimate children. In addition, he was accused of being an atheist.

Aaron Burr was named as Jefferson's running mate, and the two received the same number of votes in the election. (Electors still voted twice and there was no distinction made between votes for the first and second position in the country.) This thrust the choice of president on the House of Representatives, and the tie was not broken until the thirty-seventh ballot. At the time the House was controlled by the Federalists, and Alexander Hamilton, an enemy of Burr's, finally swayed the vote in Jefferson's favor. The disappointed Aaron Burr, who had believed that he could become the third president while Congress wrangled, challenged Hamilton to a duel and killed him.

The bitter fighting preceding Jefferson's election placed a heavy burden on the third president, and he attempted to bring about conciliation in his inaugural address. One Liverpool pitcher made during Jefferson's administration has a quotation from this speech over a portrait of the president. "We are all Republicans—all Federalists" is printed over an oval of stars intertwined with a ribbon that contains the names of the fifteen states then in existence.

73

A second Liverpool jug made during Jefferson's presidency has a less flattering portrait, and the states' names are intertwined with an olive wreath.

It was inevitable that Benjamin Franklin would be portrayed many times during his lifetime by the potters of England and France. He was a citizen of the world long before he went to France in 1776 to plead for help and financial support for his new nation. His *Poor Richard's Almanac* had already been translated into French and other languages, and his many inventions and scientific experiments were well known.

The first portraits in ceramics of Franklin were made in jasperware by Wedgwood. Josiah Wedgwood and Franklin were both concerned about the evils of slavery, and they corresponded on this and other issues of the day. Two portrait medallions were made by Wedgwood of Franklin, one showing the scientist and statesman in Roman toga and classic profile, the other depicting Franklin in his fur cap.

Fig. 95 Creamware mug with transfer of Thomas Jefferson. (SMITHSONIAN INSTITUTION PHOTOGRAPH)

*Fig. 96 Portrait medallion of Benjamin Franklin in blue and white jasper was made around 1777 by Wedgwood, who was a friend and admirer of the American philosopher.
Another medallion of Franklin, in his fur cap, was designed by Nini and made in basalt, caneware, and jasper.* (PHOTOGRAPH COURTESY JOSIAH WEDGWOOD AND SONS LIMITED)

Fig. 97 Liverpool jug to honor Benjamin Franklin. Printed in black. (MATTATUCK MUSEUM. PHOTOGRAPH BY CHARLES KLAMKIN)

Fig. 98 Reverse of Franklin jug. (MATTATUCK MUSEUM. PHOTOGRAPH BY CHARLES KLAMKIN)

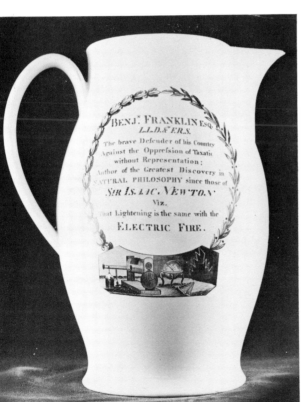

A Liverpool creamware pitcher shows an engraved copy of the painting of Franklin by John Trumbull. On the reverse side is printed:

> BENJ^N. FRANKLIN EsQ./ L.L.D. & F.R.S.
> The brave Defender of his Country
> Against the Oppression of Taxation without Representation
> Author of the Greatest Discovery in NATURAL PHILOSOPHY
> since those of SIR ISAAC NEWTON
> Viz. That Lightning is the same with the ELECTRIC FIRE.

After the War of 1812 many of the English potters manufactured cheap whiteware for the American market with engravings that illustrated the morals, proverbs, and maxims of Franklin. These were made principally for use by children, and they were generally in the form of small drinking mugs and plates of circular or octagonal shape. There were over fifty varieties of these Franklin dishes, with such educational Franklin gems as, "If you would know the value of money try to borrow some," "What maintains one vice would bring up two children," "Lost time is never found again," "Employ time well if thou meanest to gain leisure," and "It is easier to suppress the first desire than to gratify all that follow." It is highly probable that an entire generation of Americans brought up at the beginning of a new century looked upon Benjamin Franklin with something less than fond memories.

10

DESIGNS RELATING TO JAMES MADISON AND THE NAVAL BATTLES OF THE WAR OF 1812

James Madison had been the youngest delegate to the Continental Congress in 1781 and was appointed secretary of state when Thomas Jefferson entered the White House in 1801. Although Madison's duties in that position were mostly assumed by Jefferson, Jefferson did support Madison's candidacy for president in 1808. Charles Cotesworth Pinckney was the Federalist candidate whom Madison beat, by an electoral vote of 122 to 47.

The Liverpool jug in Figure 99, commemorating James Madison's presidency, is interesting from several viewpoints. The portrait is copied from a painting done by John Vanderlyn, and the engraving is quite close in appearance to the original. However, the president's last name was spelled wrong by the British engravers who were more artistic than literate. At the time the jug was made, the United States was deeply involved in European wars, and British naval officers considered every American ship at sea to be fair game. Many were boarded, their cargoes taken, and their sailors impressed into British service.

Madison's answer to this problem was to reopen trade with all nations except England and France, thus negating Jefferson's embargo. Congress gave Madison the authority to reestablish trade with both belligerent nations, considering that this would leave America free to sail and trade wherever it wished. Since neither country withdrew its edicts against American shipping, Congress restored trade with both countries in 1810, hoping that the edicts would now be revoked. This didn't happen.

Fig. 99 Liverpool pitcher with portrait of James Madison.
(SMITHSONIAN INSTITUTION)

Fig. 100 The Constitution *and the* Guerièrre. *Printed in dark blue.*
Made by Enoch Wood & Sons. (MATTATUCK MUSEUM.
PHOTOGRAPH BY CHARLES KLAMKIN)

Fig. 101 "Commodore MacDonough's Victory." Printed in dark blue. Made by Enoch Wood & Sons. (MATTATUCK MUSEUM. PHOTOGRAPH BY CHARLES KLAMKIN)

"Free trade and sailors' rights" was the cry of the anti-British factions in this country. Obviously, the Liverpool pottery merchants also believed in free trade with America. While piracy on the seas continued, at least one engraver was making decorations for a Madison creamware jug and obviously had faith that it would make the trip across the ocean.

Although the heroes of the American Revolutionary War and the patriots who helped to form our government are certainly recognizable by name, many of the heroes of the War of 1812 have long been forgotten—except for brief mention in history text books. However, the potters who made Liverpool ware to sell to American customers were quite well acquainted with the men of the first American navy and the ships that they sailed. Their portraits were considered suitable decoration for the cream colored wares.

If we have forgotten who said "Our country! In her intercourse with foreign nations may she always be in the right; but our country, right or wrong!" we need only to look at the jugs and mugs printed with the portrait of Stephen Decatur to remind us. Decatur was the son of a naval officer and went to sea as a midshipman in 1798. He became a lieutenant the following year and served in the West Indies during the undeclared war with France (1798–1801). In 1804

Fig 102 Liverpool print commemorating Commodore Preble's
achievement in Tripoli in 1804. (MATTATUCK MUSEUM.
PHOTOGRAPH BY CHARLES KLAMKIN)

Fig. 103 "Don't Surrender the Ship" was the cry
attributed to James Lawrence by the British engraver.
Printed in black with luster band around rim.
(MATTATUCK MUSEUM. PHOTOGRAPH BY CHARLES
KLAMKIN)

Fig. 104 Reverse of Lawrence pitcher had portrait of
another American naval hero, Stephen Decatur.
(MATTATUCK MUSEUM. PHOTOGRAPH BY CHARLES
KLAMKIN)

Fig. 105 Decatur mug, printed in sepia with luster band around rim. (MATTATUCK MUSEUM. PHOTOGRAPH BY CHARLES KLAMKIN)

Fig. 106 Commodore Preble Liverpool jug. Printed in black. (MATTATUCK MUSEUM. PHOTOGRAPH BY CHARLES KLAMKIN)

Fig. 107 White-glazed pitcher with luster band showing sea battle between the Enterprize and the Boxer. (MATTATUCK MUSEUM. PHOTOGRAPH BY CHARLES KLAMKIN)

Fig. 108 "Success to Trade." American ship in full sail, printed and hand-painted with gilded decoration around rim. (MAT-TATUCK MUSEUM. PHOTO-GRAPH BY CHARLES KLAM-KIN)

Fig. 109 Reverse of pitcher showing "The Farmer's Arms." (MATTATUCK MU-SEUM. PHOTOGRAPH BY CHARLES KLAMKIN)

Decatur made a daring raid on the port of Tripoli. He and his men boarded the frigate *Philadelphia*, burned it, and escaped under the fire of 141 guns. Decatur was rewarded for this exploit by being made a captain, which was then the highest rank in the navy. In the War of 1812, Decatur, commanding the frigate *United States*, captured the British frigate *Macedonian*. Early in 1815 he was captured during a battle with four British ships. Decatur was killed in 1820 in a duel with James Barron, a naval officer who had been courtmartialed and whose reinstatement as commodore Decatur opposed.

In typical British fashion, the reverse side of one Decatur pitcher has a printed portrait of another American hero of the War of 1812 with the misquote "Don't surrender the ship." This is, of course, James Lawrence, born in 1781, who was a United States naval officer. His words "Don't give up the ship!" were uttered after he had been fatally wounded, and they became a popular battle cry that was evidently heard incorrectly as far away as Liverpool.

Edward Preble is another United States naval officer whose portrait can be found on Liverpool jugs. This Falmouth, Maine, hero ran away from home at

Fig. 110 "The True Blooded Yankee" print, showing ship in full sail. (MATTATUCK MUSEUM. PHOTOGRAPH BY CHARLES KLAMKIN)

the age of sixteen to serve on a privateer. He later became a midshipman and then a lieutenant in the Massachusetts navy during the Revolutionary War. When the United States Navy was organized in 1798 Preble was made a lieutenant, and later he became a captain. He commanded the *Essex* on a cruise to the East Indies.

In 1803 Preble sailed for Tripoli on the *Constitution*, heading a squadron of seven vessels. After pirates captured the *Philadelphia*, which had preceded the squadron into the Mediterranean, Preble's men recaptured her and burned her in a daring raid. They later bombarded Tripoli, but failed to capture it. Exploits of young officers called "Preble's boys" became naval tradition.

Not only the men but the ships they sailed were fitting subjects for printed decoration on jugs commemorating the naval battles of the War of 1812. One rather well-known print, *The* Enterprise *and the* Boxer, commemorates the fierce battle between the American brig *Enterprise*, under the command of Lieutenant William Barrows, and the British man-of-war brig *Boxer*, under the command of Captain Samuel Blyth. The battle took place off shore, near Penguin Point, Maine, and resulted in many wounded sailors and considerable damage to both ships. The *Enterprise*, however, was the undisputed winner.

Fig. 111 "Come Box the Compass" prints were used in conjunction with many ship prints on Liverpool jugs. (MATTATUCK MUSEUM. PHOTOGRAPH BY CHARLES KLAMKIN)

Fig. 114 Above Modern print of ship Columbia is part of series called "The American Sailing Ship Plates" made by Wedgwood for Shreve, Crump and Low Co. of
Boston. (AUTHOR'S COLLECTION. PHOTO-
GRAPH BY CHARLES KLAMKIN)

Fig. 115 Right Mark and legend on reverse
of Columbia plate.

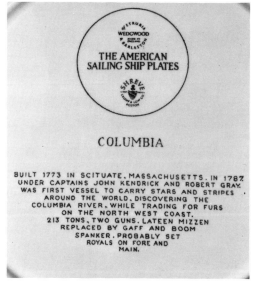

Another naval battle that is almost better known for the fact that it is commemorated on a Liverpool pitcher than for its historical importance took place off the shore of Stonington, Connecticut, during the War of 1812. An inscription on this large (12 1/2-inch) pitcher reads "The Gallant Defense of Stonington, Connecticut, August 9th, 1814. Stonington is free whilst her Heroes have one gun left." The town of Stonington was attacked on that day by the British navy,

Fig. 116 "Flying Cloud" by Wedgwood. New version of old engravings of famous nineteenth-century American clipper ships. Printed in red. (PHOTOGRAPH COURTESY OF JOSIAH WEDGWOOD AND SONS LIMITED)

and the citizens of the town resisted and sank one British ship. Examples of the jug, made in the Herculaneum Pottery of Liverpool, can be found in several museum collections. The example in Plate 4 is transfer printed in black and has gilding and colored enamel decoration as well. It was made around 1815.

Sailing ships were, of course, a rather common decoration for Liverpool ware that was sold to sailors. Many of these ship motifs are accompanied by the message "Success to Trade." The city of Liverpool badly needed American trade at the end of the hostilities between the two countries, and the British potters were not embarrassed to admit it openly on their wares.

Besides those heroes and sea battles of the War of 1812 that are mentioned above, the battles betwen the *Hornet* and the *Bonne Atoyenne*, the *Hornet* and the *Peacock*, and the *Wasp* and the *Frolic*, and the battles on Lake Erie and Lake Champlain have all been commemorated by British pottery decorators. In their zeal to make and decorate wares that would appeal to their postwar customers, the Liverpool potters, who, after all, lived in a seaport town and must have lost many of their citizens in these battles for supremacy over American waters, were most certainly not sore losers.

11

DESIGNS RELATING TO JAMES MONROE AND THE VISIT OF GENERAL LAFAYETTE

James Monroe, who seems to have been ignored by the engravers who decorated Liverpool pitchers, was the third consecutive Democratic-Republican president of the United States. He began his administration by touring the northern United States in the hope of establishing national unity. He was received by cheering crowds in every city and town he visited, and the "era of good feelings" became the label for Monroe's administration. A new feeling of patriotism and nationalism developed following the War of 1812.

James Monroe had had a long career in politics before he became president in 1817. He fought and was wounded in the Revolutionary War and he was a close friend of Lafayette, whose wounds he had treated. Thomas Jefferson, who had taken Monroe on as a law student, was also a lifelong friend. Monroe entered political life in 1782 as a member of the Virginia Assembly. He was a member of the Continental Congress and ran for Congress against James Madison in 1788, but was defeated. He became the United States senator from Virginia in 1790 and during the next four years was instrumental in consolidating anti-Federalist factions into the Democratic-Republican party. In 1794 Monroe was sent as the American minister to France. His task was to smooth relations with that country, which felt that the alliance between the United States and England was too strong. Washington recalled Monroe when it became apparent that he favored the side of the French too strongly and did not represent the will of the American government.

In 1799 James Monroe was elected governor of Virginia, and in 1803 he was again sent to France, this time by President Jefferson to negotiate a treaty with the French for free navigation of the Mississippi River. However, by the time Monroe got to Paris, Robert Livingston had already arranged the Louisiana Purchase, and Monroe was ordered to Spain in what was to be a futile attempt to acquire Spanish Florida. Monroe was then asked to go to England to make an attempt to straighten out our shipping problems with that country.

James Monroe was elected to the Virginia legislature in 1810, and in 1811 he was again made governor of that state. Shortly after taking that office, he was appointed secretary of state. In 1814, as secretary of war, a position he now held simultaneously with his other office, Monroe reorganized the Department of War. Having had great success in his role as secretary of war, Monroe became a natural choice for the presidential nomination in 1816. He won the election from Rufus King by an electoral vote of 183 to 34.

Although there are no Liverpool pitchers that honor James Monroe directly, many of the designs for engravings for the jugs are indicative of the history of Monroe's administration. Also, since Monroe was instrumental in bringing his old friend General Lafayette to these shores for a year-long visit in 1824, he was indirectly responsible for all the Lafayette souvenir items made during the final year of his administration.

A singular event took place in the year 1824–1825 that unified the nation and led to a year-long celebration that the United States would long remember. In that year General Lafayette, by this time the only Revolutionary War general still alive, came to these shores as the guest of the president and Congress. In his old age Lafayette somehow found the strength to travel throughout the United States and to visit every principal city and territory. It was said that there was hardly a citizen living that year who did not lay eyes on Lafayette at least once.

Wherever the hero visited, souvenirs were sold, and many gifts were given to Lafayette to commemorate the occasion. Blue and white earthenware was at the height of its popularity at this time, and the British potters did not hesitate to produce souvenir plates and whole sets of dishes and teaware commemorating the visit of Lafayette. Lafayette's entire tour of America can be traced in the motifs of the British printed plates that still exist. America as seen by Lafayette can now be seen by us in the blue and white motifs used as plate decoration. Plates made during Lafayette's visit present a fairly complete picture of our cities, their buildings, the sailing ships that took Lafayette to and from this continent,

Fig. 117 "Landing of Gen. LaFayette at Castle Garden, New York." Printed in dark blue. Made by Clews. (MATTATUCK MUSEUM. PHOTOGRAPH BY CHARLES KLAMKIN)

Fig. 118 Cadmus at anchor. Ship that brought Lafayette to America in 1824. Printed in dark blue. Made by Enoch Wood & Sons. (MATTATUCK MUSEUM. PHOTOGRAPH BY CHARLES KLAMKIN)

Fig. 119 Creamware plate with bust portrait of Lafayette. Printed in dark blue. Embossed rim on plate. Maker unknown. (MATTATUCK MUSEUM. PHOTOGRAPH BY CHARLES KLAMKIN)

Fig. 120 East view of LaGrange, Lafayette's home outside of Paris. Printed in dark blue. Made by Enoch Wood & Sons. (MATTATUCK MUSEUM. PHOTOGRAPH BY CHARLES KLAMKIN)

our monuments to dead heroes, and, in a few cases, the British version of the reception given to Lafayette as his ship approached these shores. As usual, the British potters were aware of events taking place in America and were always ready to produce whatever they thought Americans would purchase.

The visit of General Lafayette, as seen on old blue and white printed plates, began with the French hero's landing at Castle Garden in New York on August 16, 1824. His sailing vessel, the *Cadmus*, was the property of an American merchant and had been placed at Lafayette's disposal after he had refused an offer by President Monroe to send a government ship for the journey. Lafayette's son, George Washington Lafayette, and the General's secretary, A. Levasseur, accompanied the hero on his voyage. It is to Lafayette's secretary that we owe what information there is about the year Lafayette spent touring America. His rather complete journal of the year-long, arduous visit was published in France and America in 1826.

Fig. 121 Platter showing full front view of LaGrange. Printed in dark blue. Made by Enoch Wood & Sons. (MATTATUCK MUSEUM. PHOTOGRAPH BY CHARLES KLAMKIN)

94

Fig. 122 Erie Canal plate. Made to honor DeWitt Clinton and opening of canal. Printed in medium blue. Maker unknown. (MATTATUCK MUSEUM. PHOTOGRAPH BY CHARLES KLAMKIN)

The *Cadmus* took fifteen days to arrive at Castle Garden, New York, from France, and cannon from Fort Lafayette boomed a welcome on the Sunday that the ship put into shore. The party observed the Sabbath at the home of Vice President Daniel D. Tompkins, on Staten Island, so the real welcome took place on the following day. The scene of the welcome as depicted by the British engravers can be found on a plate inscribed "Landing of General Lafayette at Castle Garden, August 16, 1824." This is probably a rather accurate picture of how the harbor looked that day. Castle Garden was connected to the Battery by a 300-foot bridge. Decorated ships filled the harbor, and three of the newly invented steamboats welcomed the general and his party. Two of the ships, the *Fulton* and the *Chancellor Livingston*, can both be identified in the engraving. Two hundred thousand people greeted the general as he landed and was taken by carriage to City Hall. The New York buildings that he saw along his route were all subjects of printed blue and white plates. The City Hotel on Broadway, in which Lafayette lived while in New York, is also the subject of printed plates.

Great celebrations were held in every city that Lafayette visited. A Grand Fete was held at Castle Garden, during which a huge transparency of La Grange, Lafayette's home outside of Paris, was flashed on the wall. La Grange is the subject of several plates made to commemorate the visit.

From New York, Lafayette and his group traveled to Boston, where he paid homage to the heroes of the battles of Lexington and Bunker Hill. Later in that year Lafayette laid the cornerstone for the Bunker Hill monument. At a banquet, held at Harvard during this visit and attended by 1,500 citizens, the centerpiece consisted of war relics picked up on the Bunker Hill battlefield.

From Boston, the troup went to Hartford, where the children from the newly constructed deaf and dumb asylum, the first institution of its kind to be built in America, greeted Lafayette by pointing to a huge banner inscribed "What others express, we feel."

Lafayette then went to New Haven and Yale College, and thence on to New York, where a steamboat, the *James Kent*, carried him up the Hudson River to Tarrytown. At West Point Lafayette reviewed the cadets and, as was true everywhere, was greeted by an enormous crowd. The next landing place was Poughkeepsie, and, after spending the night at the home of Chancellor Livingston, the general again boarded the boat and continued up the Hudson River to the village of Catskill. At a stop in Albany, DeWitt Clinton, former governor of New York and champion of the Erie Canal, boarded ship and accompanied Lafayette to Troy.

Following his return to New York, Lafayette set out on a journey through the southern and western states. There he was celebrated in every town and pre-

Fig. 123 Reproduction of earlier Washington pitcher made during first quarter of this century, probably to honor 100th anniversary of Lafayette's visit. Unmarked. (DEWITT COLLECTION, UNIVERSITY OF HARTFORD. PHOTOGRAPH BY CHARLES KLAMKIN)

Fig. 124 Print of Washington is on reverse of Lafayette pitcher. This print, for obvious reasons, is called "The Ugly Washington." (DEWITT COLLECTION, UNIVERSITY OF HARTFORD. PHOTOGRAPH BY CHARLES KLAMKIN)

sented with hundreds of gifts from people along the route. An enormous celebration was held when Lafayette visited Philadelphia. During this "era of good feelings," Lafayette was given credit for everything good that had happened during the nation's struggle for independence. Poems and songs were written in his honor, and infant industries vied with one another to produce souvenirs befitting the occasion of his visit. It is interesting that the most graphic of these mementos of the year-long celebration are the engraved plates manufactured by the British.

One event that appealed to the sentimental natures of British plate decorators was the visit of Lafayette to the tomb of his friend and mentor, George Washington. During the year, Lafayette had managed to visit each of the three former presidents still alive at the time: John Adams, who, at eighty-nine years of age, was living in Quincy, Massachusetts; Thomas Jefferson, who had retired to Monticello; and James Madison, whom Lafayette visited at Montpelier. None of these visits stirred the pottery decorators' imaginations as much as Lafayette's sentimental visit to Washington's tomb. The print showing Lafayette in a mournful pose near the tomb of his friend was probably the most popular of all the blue and white pottery relics.

During his year in America, it is probable that not one new monument built in memory of the heroes of the Revolution and the War of 1812 was missed by Lafayette. Every new public building was the cause for a visit and often for a series of speeches. Niagara Falls was seen by the Frenchman, and he managed to visit the Erie Canal shortly before "Clinton's Ditch" was completed and dedicated.

To the British potters goes the credit for preserving Lafayette's historic visit in pictures. While it is probable that some of the views of buildings and monuments had, before his visit, been the subjects of blue and white plates, the subjects that could be connected with Lafayette's visit were made and sold in quantity during the year 1824–1825 and for many years thereafter. It is typical of the sentimentality and patriotism of the period that Americans were content to pour their cream out of pitchers that depicted a grieving Lafayette at the tomb of Washington for many years following the event pictured.

While it is true that many of the scenes found on blue and white earthenware plates made for the American market are sentimental and obviously not very accurate in detail, in many instances the plates are the only record we have of how things looked in those early days of the Republic. Judging from the number of plates that have survived, it is also probable that few Americans were not reminded three times a day that Lafayette *was* here.

12

JOHN QUINCY ADAMS
AND ANDREW JACKSON
CHINA

It is no surprise that the British potters chose to ignore John Quincy Adams's presidency. Adams had no love for England, his prejudice stemming from his having witnessed as a child the battle at Bunker Hill. Adams was, of course, the son of our second president and was extremely well traveled and well educated by the time he was elected to the Massachusetts legislature in 1802.

Throughout his early career John Quincy Adams was under constant attack for his refusal to align himself strongly with his party, the Federalists. Because of his independence in supporting issues beyond party lines, Adams was forced to resign his seat in the legislature after three years. It was unfashionable in New England at that time not to be an Anglophile, and Adams was far from that. The War of 1812 proved to many that his prejudices had been justified.

James Monroe appointed Adams in 1809 as minister to Russia, and in 1814 he was sent to Ghent, where he and others signed a treaty with England on December 21. Following this, Adams was sent to England as minister to the Court of St. James. This was a strange appointment for an anti-British states-man, but Adams stayed until he was appointed secretary of state in 1817.

John Quincy Adams's record as secretary of state under James Monroe was brilliant. Unlike Jefferson, Monroe believed in delegating responsibilities to his cabinet members. Adams worked extremely hard in this position and put aside his prejudice to negotiate alliances with England that set a foundation for the friendly alliance between the two countries.

Fig. 126 Creamware cup plate with transfer of Andrew Jackson in sepia print. Rimmed in brown enamel.

(MR. AND MRS. LEON WEISSEL. PHOTOGRAPH BY CHARLES KLAMKIN)

Fig. 125 Redware tile with standing portrait of John Quincy Adams. (SMITHSONIAN INSTITUTION PHOTOGRAPH)

Fig. 127 Right "Jackson, Hero of New Orleans." Creamware plate. (SMITHSONIAN INSTITUTION. PHOTOGRAPH BY CHARLES KLAMKIN)

Adams had a strong desire to become president after Monroe. The only existing party at the time was the Democratic-Republican party, and there were four candidates for the election: Secretary of the Treasury William H. Crawford, Senator Henry Clay, General Andrew Jackson, and John Quincy Adams. Andrew Jackson led the balloting with 99 votes and Adams was second with 84 electoral votes. But Jackson had received 40,000 more popular votes than Adams. However, none of the candidates had received a majority. Henry Clay, after what must have been a great deal of soul-searching, threw his 37 electoral votes to Adams, and the House of Representatives declared Adams the winner only three weeks before inauguration. Adams appointed Henry Clay as secretary of state, and the charge that a political deal had been made followed Adams throughout his administration.

An appropriate ceramic memento of John Quincy Adams' administration is the pipe head commemorating Henry Clay, in Figure 66. Another rare ceramic object is a redware plaque (Figure 125) commemorating John Quincy Adams, which has a figure of the president and the words "Peace, Prosperity, Home Industry, J. Q. Adams" embossed on it.

Fig. 128 This printed portrait, called "Genl. Jackson, Hero of America," is really a picture of Lafayette as a young man. On one rare Liverpool print Thomas Jefferson is extolled, but the portrait is of King George III. Luster band. (MR. AND MRS. LEON WEISSEL. PHOTOGRAPH BY CHARLES KLAMKIN)

Fig. 129 Portrait of General Andrew Jackson is printed on this pitcher banded with luster. (SMITHSONIAN IN-STITUTION PHOTOGRAPH)

Andrew Jackson, having lost his first bid to become president to John Quincy Adams, easily won the election in 1828. Adams didn't even wait for Jackson's inauguration, but left town the night before. It was just as well, since he might have been trampled by the crowds of people who came to see the inauguration of the first "people's president." The president himself was almost trod upon by the mob that stampeded the White House.

Andrew Jackson symbolized to middle-class America the American Dream. He had been born in frontier country and had struggled to attain glory and power. He was "the hero of New Orleans," having been credited with saving that city in a daring counterattack on the British. Further exploits in acquiring land in Florida for the United States endeared him to rural America, and politicians saw him as good presidential material. Jackson was appointed to the Senate in 1823 and ran for president the following year. After Clay threw his votes to Adams, Jackson resigned his Senate seat and began to campaign for the next presidential election. Jackson's supporters blocked Adams' programs wherever they could, and Jackson's four-year political campaign is one of the basest on record for that time. His wife Rachel, who opposed Jackson's candidacy on the grounds that she never saw him and that his health would not tolerate the strenuous duties of the presidency, was the object of the worst smear campaign that has ever been waged in the history of American politics. She had been married previously to a Lewis Robards, and the marriage had not been legally terminated before she married Jackson. Neither Jackson nor Rachel knew until after they were married that there had been no legal divorce, and much against Jackson's will, but to stop gossip, the two had a second wedding ceremony. Gossip and slander concerning the affair became a campaign issue, however, and, broken-hearted and ailing, Rachel died on December 17, 1828.

Jackson, who won in his second attempt to become president of the United States by an electoral vote of 178 to 83, never forgave his enemies for the vicious slander that his beloved Rachel had endured and swore never to forgive her "murderers." Jackson himself had been maligned along with his wife in the foul campaign, and he entered the White House an embittered man.

The popularity of Jackson and the length of his stay in the White House gave British potters time and cause to make many commemorative relics. One particularly amusing pitcher, probably made before Jackson became president, is a luster pitcher (see Plate 9) that has an engraving of Lafayette as a young man and the words "Gen. Jackson, Hero of America" above the portrait. On another early luster pitcher a true portrait of Jackson is used, with the legend, "General Jackson, The Hero of New Orleans." A small, rare creamware cup plate (see Figure 126) has just a portrait of the president.

Fig. 130 American pottery crock. Dark brown glaze. Made in honor of General Jackson's election. (SMITHSONIAN INSTITUTION PHOTOGRAPH)

13

ANTISLAVERY CHINA

The problem of slavery in the United States has been the subject of at least three ceramic objects, one of which was made as early as 1786 by Josiah Wedgwood. A cameo in black and white jasper, modeled by William Hackwood for Wedgwood, pictures a kneeling slave in chains and the motto "Am I not a Man and a Brother?" Adopted by the Committee of the Society for the Abolition of Slavery as its seal on October 16, 1787, this medallion has been reproduced many times by the Wedgwood firm, and copied by many other ceramics firms. In the early part of the nineteenth century it was distributed in quantity to British and American citizens who were against slavery, and the cameo was set into rings, shirt pins, buttons, brooches, and so forth. The early cameos made by Wedgwood were not marked.

An antislavery plate was made by a Staffordshire potter around 1837, shortly after the death of Elijah Parish Lovejoy, the abolitionist editor of the *St. Louis Observer* who was persecuted and finally killed by a proslavery mob. According to Alice Morse Earle, who wrote *China Collecting in America* in 1892, the Staffordshire plate commemorating Lovejoy had by that time become extremely popular among collectors.

The design of the antislavery plate was printed in a light purplish blue, and along with the plate various other shapes in tea and dinner services were printed with the same motif. The original plates were the gift of the English Anti-Slavery Society to the American abolitionists. They were sold at auction in New York, and the proceeds were donated to aid the causes of the Society of Abolitionists.

In the border of the antislavery plate are four cartouches. The one at the top of the plate contains the words "The Tyrant's Foe—The People's Friend."

Fig. 131 "First Amendment Plate," also called the "Antislavery plate," is printed in medium blue. Maker unknown. (MATTATUCK MUSEUM. PHOTOGRAPH BY CHARLES KLAMKIN)

Fig. 132 Josiah Wedgwood's slave medallions were set into many different kinds of jewelery and were fashionable among antislavery factions in the eighteenth century. (PHOTOGRAPH COURTESY OF JOSIAH WEDGWOOD AND SONS LIMITED)

In the left cartouche is printed "We hold that all Men are Created Equal," and in the right, "Of One Blood are all Nations." In the center of the plate, against a sunburst background, are the words "Congress shall make no law respecting an establishment of religion or prohibiting the free exercise thereof; or abridging the freedom of speech, or of the press, or the right to assemble and to petition the government for a redress of grievances. Constitution U. S."

Designs of the American eagle and stars are seen in the border. In the bottom medallion is the design of the scales of justice, and the cartouche at the top of the border contains the figure of Liberty standing beside a printing press with a slave in chains kneeling at her feet. It was obviously necessary, after the tragedy of Lovejoy, for the British to remind Americans of the words of their Constitution and the rights of their citizens.

The antislavery plate was immediately popular among American collectors, and the attention brought to it by Mrs. Earle in 1892 caused the price to go so high that forgers made new tributes to Lovejoy. These reproductions, made around 1897, were sold as genuine originals, for from fifteen to thirty dollars apiece. However, the reproductions are thicker than the original plates, which were light and porous.

The antislavery plates were somewhat easier to reproduce than the dark blue and white historical plates of the earlier period. The originals were unmarked, and according to Edwin Atlee Barber, who discussed the reproductions in 1899 in *Anglo—American Pottery*, they were "the rarest design [for forging] that occurred in a color most easily copied and which were not marked with a maker's name."

When British potters did comment on American politics through the medium of pottery or porcelain, they rarely signed their names or marked their wares in any manner on the reverse sides. This is one reason why there is a mystery surrounding who produced the antislavery plate in Plate 10 and when. It bears the Hackwood-designed medallion of the "Slave in Chains" as a center motif. It is porcelain rather than earthenware and is cream colored. The Wedgwood firm was making bone china of this type and shape for a short period around 1820, and it is possible that this rare plate is a product of that firm.

14

AMERICAN POLITICAL CHINA

The patriotic and political printed plates that were made in such great quantities in England for the American market overshadowed those made by the pottery industry on American soil. When good quality pottery was produced here, it was usually the work of an immigrant Staffordshire potter who had been carefully trained in his own country. The competition for the sale of plates was too strong for the aspiring American potters, and in the category of mass-produced printed tableware there is little doubt that the British owned the American market. Despite the many efforts of small potteries in America to manufacture dinnerware that would appeal to fellow Americans, there was a great deal of resistance in the marketplace to ceramics made domestically. Many of the American potters used marks that were adaptations or direct copies of foreign pottery and porcelain marks.

Despite the fact that quite a few small potteries were already in operation by 1840 in the United States, the process for printing on ceramics was not used until that year. One of the earliest examples of American printed earthenware is the Harrison pitcher in Figure 138. Two centers in the United States where pottery industries were successfully run during the first half of the nineteenth century are Trenton, New Jersey, and East Liverpool, Ohio. Clay, fuel, and convenient transportation were available in both places, but prior to the Civil War little innovative work was done. The object of American potters during that period was to produce wares cheaply that were close copies of British ceramics. Very little was made that was either shaped in American patriotic motifs or decorated in a manner similar to the dark blue and white plates.

The Benjamin Harrison pitcher, of which several versions were made, was in the tradition of the British patriotic earthenware. Throughout the history of the many political campaigns for the American presidency, thousands of plates have been made and decorated with slogans for, or pictures of, the candidates. In the past, it was far more simple to make the candidate's name a household word when a plate bearing his portrait hung on the kitchen wall. The potters usually played no favorites, and matching plates with the opposing candidates' likenesses can be found for many elections. Party emblems and campaign slogans were sometimes used as plate decoration prior to an election. Many items were also made of ceramics to be used as favors at fund-raising dinners and rallies.

Obviously, when a plate is to be decorated for use as campaign material, quality is the last thing that the purchasers are interested in. The quality of campaign pottery or porcelain has seldom been important. Therefore, all American political china has been considered junk by those collectors interested only in ceramics, and campaign china appeals mainly to people who collect American political items. Since many of these plates were made on speculation by the

Fig. 133 Even though Winfield Scott's image is shown on an alphabet plate, his name is spelled wrong. He was Whig presidential candidate in 1852 and was defeated by Franklin Pierce. (MR. AND MRS. LEON WEISSEL. PHOTOGRAPH BY CHARLES KLAMKIN)

potters themselves, many of them are not, strictly speaking, campaign material. That is, they were not sold or given away by the organization that the candidate represented. Even when these earthenware objects were given out as campaign material, no records can be found today to verify that fact.

Arguments given by ceramics collectors as to why these plates are worthless in their collections usually have to do with the fact that the china is of poor quality. In many cases, however, this is not so. Before 1900 most of the American political plates came from Germany or France and were imported undecorated. There were many firms in this country that specialized in plate decoration and sales only, and the political portraits and motifs were applied in this country.

One rather important plate decorating firm was Haughwout & Daily, which went into business before the Civil War. This New York firm had its establishment at 561 and 563 Broadway and employed about fifty painters, who decorated French china imported in blanks. Plates could be decorated to order in a short period of time by this firm, and specially designed plates were made for the White House during the Pierce, Buchanan, and Lincoln administrations. The same firm decorated candy dishes and other plates with eagle motifs for sale to the general public. Since the decorating firm did not mark the plates they decorated, it is impossible today to tell which of the pre–Civil War patriotic plates were designed and decorated by them. This is also true of the many other smaller plate-decorating firms operating in the United States at that time.

Of the campaign and political china made during the period from 1855 to the end of the nineteenth century, few of the plates can be traced to their manufacturers or decorators. There is, however, one very great advantage to owning political china: It is usually a fairly simple matter to tell *when* the plates were made.

Most of the political portrait plates were made following the centennial celebration in Philadelphia in 1876. By this time some large potteries had been established in America, and the most innovative pottery and porcelain from all over the world, much of which was shown at the centennial exhibit, encouraged the American potters. The taste in America for all-over decorated plates had been abandoned for more simple tableware, but it was not felt to be in poor taste to have a portrait of one's favorite political candidate on a china pin tray or on a plate that was used just for show. By this time, the invention of a lithograph method for transferring colorful designs to ceramics had made it even easier and cheaper to make red, white, and blue motifs to represent the political parties.

Not only the presidential candidates, but the also-rans, and the vice presidents can be found on the plates from this prolific period.

The prototype for the political portrait plates can be found in the souvenir ceramics that historically have been made in England at the time of a coronation or other important royal events. However, American presidential campaigns are held every four years, and there is a great amount more of this sort of commemorative china for the American collector than there is of its British prototype. Where quality was secondary, quantity, especially in the case of a few candidates who had great financial backing for their campaigns, was ample. However, since little was thought of these portrait plates once the candidate had lost an election and faded into oblivion or had won and been in office long enough to disillusion even some of his most faithful campaigners, not too many have been preserved.

Patriotic and political plates of the second hundred years of our history will be of similar importance to the Liverpool jugs and the dark blue and white Staffordshire that is so highly prized by collectors today. The men whose portraits appear on the later plates are no less important to our history than were our early patriots and presidents. Any items that record our history are worth preserving, no matter what the quality or intrinsic value of the material from which they are made. Some of the earliest political portrait plates are the only dated examples we have of American fictile art.

Patriotic and political china of the latter half of the nineteenth century and of the twentieth century will take its place with the earlier wares made by the British potters for this market. Earthenware is one of the least ephemeral materials on which political slogans and candidates' portraits can appear. Campaign banners and posters and other inexpensive items related to our political campaigns are frequently thrown away once the excitement of the event is over. One might put a plate away in a drawer, but it is very difficult to throw out an unbroken plate. It is to be hoped that more than just the campaign and political china which is illustrated here will be dusted off and preserved for future historians and collectors.

15

DESIGNS RELATING TO WILLIAM HENRY HARRISON AND ZACHARY TAYLOR

Although no presidential candidate after George Washington was without some rival for office, the British potters could freely manufacture printed jugs and plates extolling the virtues of the next five presidents with the assurance that a wide market would be found for those wares in the United States. As has been mentioned, the heroes of the War of 1812 were felt by the British potters to be fitting subjects for adulation. It was not, however, until the campaign for the presidency in 1840 that the infant ceramics industry in New Jersey was moved to manufacture an item of political importance.

William Henry Harrison was defeated in his campaign for the presidency in 1836 by Martin Van Buren. In 1840 Harrison was nominated by the Whig party and elected president after a long, loud, and bitter campaign that was the beginning of political campaigns as we know them today. Harrison is remembered more for his second campaign for the presidency than he is for his short term in that office. Name calling, political slogans, and symbolic devices that would immediately conjure up feelings for or against the candidates were all part of the Harrison–Van Buren political battle in 1840.

Harrison's father was a wealthy tobacco planter and a signer of the Declaration of Independence. However, in order to establish Harrison as an exponent of democratic simplicity, those responsible for his campaign circulated the story that Harrison came from more simple origins. Van Buren was labeled an aristocrat, with little understanding of the wishes of the common people, and it was some-

Fig. 134 William Harrison campaign in 1840 was first political campaign to be commemorated on large amounts of printed earthenware. "Log Cabin" print on pierced vegetable plate showing horse and man with plough in front of cabin. (MR. AND MRS. LEON WEISSEL. PHOTOGRAPH BY CHARLES KLAMKIN)

Fig. 135 Log cabin printed plate, showing man in front of cabin. Made for political campaign of William Harrison. (DEWITT COLLECTION, UNIVERSITY OF HARTFORD. PHOTOGRAPH BY CHARLES KLAMKIN)

how rumored that Harrison had grown up in a log cabin. A Philadelphia reporter stated that if one settled a small pension on the candidate and kept him supplied with a barrel of cider he would settle in his log cabin and stop campaigning. This charge was taken up by Harrison's opposition, but was turned to advantage by the Whigs. Log cabins, often with cider barrels to quench the thirst of other "common men," were built as campaign headquarters in many cities. The American flag was flown from the roofs of these makeshift offices. The symbols of the cabin, flag, and cider barrel began to appear on many campaign items. Glass whiskey flasks, ceramic plates and other objects, posters, broadsides, and badges all bore log cabin and cider barrel motifs. The modern political campaign with all its name calling and ballyhoo was born.

Harrison's campaign was a difficult one. The cry "Van, Van's a used up man" was heard during the speech making and parades. As it turned out, this epithet boomeranged for Harrison. The campaign was so hard on him that he lived only one month after having taken office. Ironically, Harrison was very much in debt at the time of his death, and had he not won the election, it is probable that he would not have been able to afford even the log cabin. The first pension ever granted to a president's widow was voted by Congress to Mrs. Harrison after her husband's death.

Fig. 136 Child's tea set was made with Harrison log cabin motifs. Plates were printed in variety of colors. (DEWITT COLLECTION, UNIVERSITY OF HARTFORD. PHOTOGRAPH BY CHARLES KLAMKIN)

William Henry Harrison, who had been a major general in the army, was the subject of much ceramic decoration. His political symbols, log cabin and cider barrel, can be found printed on tea sets and dinner plates made in England at the time of his campaign. However, the most interesting ceramic relic from Harrison's campaign is the pitcher made and decorated by the American Pottery Manufacturing Company of Jersey City. This pitcher was described in 1892 by Alice Morse Earle as

six-sided, bulging in the middle to a diameter of about nine inches, about eleven inches in height, and with a foliated handle and scalloped lip. It was of coarse-grained brownish pottery, darker in shade than Liverpool ware. On four of its sides the pitcher bore a view of a small log-cabin above a good portrait of Harrison, with the words, "The Ohio Farmer W. H. Harrison." Below all, a spread eagle. On the bottom of the pitcher was printed in black, "Am. Pottery Manf^y Co., Jersey City.

Mrs. Morse asserted that it was the only piece of American ware that she had ever seen with printed decorations similar to Liverpool ware.

John Ridgway of Staffordshire also manufactured Harrison printed earthenware for the American market. One of the Harrison patterns, which is bordered in large stars upon a firmament of smaller ones, is called "Columbian Star" and is dated October 28, 1840. There were several different log cabin designs engraved by Thomas Hordley for Ridgway. One is an end view of the cabin with two men in the drawing; another is a side view; still another has the cabin, with a man driving a horse and plow in the foreground. The patterns were produced in light blue, black, brown, or red. By this time the dark blue that had previously been used on printed ware made for the American market was going out of style. The log cabin patterns obviously appealed to American patriotism, and the plates originally designed for political purposes were popular long after Harrison had departed the White House and the world.

There were few, if any, ceramic tributes paid to Martin Van Buren, John Tyler, or James Knox Polk. However, Zachary Taylor inspired at least one china mug on which is engraved his rugged likeness. The reverse side of the mug has a portrait of Washington (see Figure 139). It is probable that the mug was a campaign item, since Taylor is described as "General Taylor" under the portrait.

Zachary Taylor was a national hero when he was elected to office in 1848. He lived only sixteen months after taking office, but his inauguration drew the largest crowd ever to be seen in the capital, and these same crowds returned to mourn him at his funeral. Taylor was, like Jackson, a man of the people and had

Fig. 137 Plate, made and printed in America with motifs of William Harrison and log cabin print in center. (MR. AND MRS. LEON WEISSEL. PHOTOGRAPH BY CHARLES KLAMKIN)

Fig. 138 Log cabin pitcher for Harrison's campaign in 1840. One of earliest examples of printed china made in America. Black prints. Jersey City Pottery, 1840. (PHOTOGRAPH FROM Anglo-American Pottery BY EDWIN ATLEE BARBER, 1901)

been brought up on a frontier settlement near Louisville, Kentucky. A farmer, Taylor became a successful career soldier and was a hero during the Mexican War. President Polk, realizing he was threat to the presidency, had him replaced in Mexico by General Winfield Scott, then army chief of staff. Taylor, realizing he had been victimized by Polk and Scott, disobeyed orders and marched his troops to Monterey, even though he was aware that he was outnumbered by the enemy four to one. He fought the Mexicans and lost over seven hundred men, but he caused Santa Anna to retreat that night. This, and his previous feats of daring on the battlefield, caused Taylor to become the idol of the American people. Eventually, after much pleading from his supporters, Taylor agreed to run for the presidency on the Whig ticket.

Millard Fillmore, vice president under Taylor, filled in for the remainder of the old soldier's term. Fillmore, often referred to as "the forgotten President," doesn't seem to have been remembered by any ceramics producers either.

Fig. 139 Zachary Taylor white ironstone china mug. Reverse has print of George Washington. Printed in black. (MR. AND MRS. LEON WEISSEL. PHOTOGRAPH BY CHARLES KLAMKIN)

16

DESIGNS RELATING TO ABRAHAM LINCOLN ANDREW JOHNSON, AND ULYSSES S. GRANT

Neither Franklin Pierce nor his successor, James Buchanan, seemed to inspire the manufacture of plates or any other ceramic objects carrying their likenesses. However, our sixteenth president is still the subject of busts, plaques, and other ceramic tributes to his memory. Our martyred presidents are never without their monuments, and ceramics manufacturers can usually fill this need before anyone else. Abraham Lincoln, bearded or smooth-shaven, is, next to George Washington, the most modeled president of the United States.

Parian and basalt busts made by Wedgwood and other British potters, and bas-relief tablets of Lincoln, have always been popular in America. Any anniversary of Lincoln's birth, death, or presidential election has been the reason for a new issue of Lincoln memorabilia. Because Lincoln's assassination brought about the manufacture of hundreds of souvenir items, it is impossible to tell whether or not any of the existing ceramic objects were made during the president's lifetime. One interesting object, the creamware pitcher in Figure 145, shows Lincoln delivering his Gettysburg Address to a crowd of top-hatted citizens. Lincoln's image is also included on later "Our Martyred Heroes" plates and other objects (see Plates 28, 30), along with McKinley and Garfield, all victims of assassins' bullets.

The portrait plate of Lincoln (see Plate 11) was quite possibly made during the president's administration. A plate associated with Lincoln's administration, and contemporary with it, is the one in Figure 146, showing a portrait of a for-

Fig. 140 Pair of Victorian-style flare vases with portraits of Lincoln and Grant.
(DEWITT COLLECTION, UNIVERSITY OF HARTFORD. PHOTOGRAPH BY CHARLES KLAMKIN)

Fig. 141 Lincoln commemorative plate decorated by amateur artist at beginning of this century. (DEWITT COLLECTION, UNIVERSITY OF HARTFORD. PHOTOGRAPH BY CHARLES KLAMKIN)

Fig. 142 American vase with raised bust portrait of Lincoln, surrounded by wreath, with eagle at top. Brown glaze. (DEWITT COLLECTION, UNIVERSITY OF HARTFORD. PHOTOGRAPH BY CHARLES KLAMKIN)

Fig. 143 Small Parian bust of a young, beardless Abe Lincoln. (DEWITT COLLECTION, UNIVERSITY OF HARTFORD. PHOTOGRAPH BY CHARLES KLAMKIN)

Fig. 144 In this miniature Parian bust, Lincoln is older—and bearded. (DEWITT COLLECTION, UNIVERSITY OF HARTFORD. PHOTOGRAPH BY CHARLES KLAMKIN)

Fig. 145 Gravy boat with print of Lincoln delivering Gettysburg Adress. (DEWITT COLLECTION, UNIVERSITY OF HARTFORD. PHOTOGRAPH BY CHARLES KLAMKIN)

Fig. 146 Modern basalt bust made by Wedgwood. One of a limited edtiion. (PHOTOGRAPH COURTESY OF JOSIAH WEDGWOOD AND SONS LIMITED)

Fig. 147 Hannibal Hamlin was Lincoln's running mate in the election of 1860. His radical approach to the question of slavery caused him not to be renominated. (MR. AND MRS. LEON WEISSEL. PHOTOGRAPH BY CHARLES KLAMKIN)

Fig. 148 Souvenir plate from home of Andrew Johnson. Printed in blue on white earthenware. (DR. EDMUND SULLIVAN)

Fig. 149 Alphabet plate with print in black of Ulysses S. Grant. Plate made in Staffordshire. (SMITHSONIAN INSTITUTION PHOTOGRAPH)

gotten man, Hannibal Hamlin, who was Lincoln's running mate in the election of 1860. Hamlin, who disagreed with Lincoln's conservative approach to the problem of emancipation during his first term, was not nominated a second time, and Andrew Johnson became Lincoln's second vice president.

The period of the Civil War was not conducive to much in the way of decorative or commemorative china. A white china vase, owned by a descendant of Andrew Johnson, is a souvenir of the Lincoln-Johnson inauguration in 1865 and has sepia printed portraits of the candidates on either side. A white china and brass coffee maker in the shape of a train is owned by the Smithsonian Institution. It is monogrammed in gold with the name of "President Jefferson Davis" and was purchased by Andrew Johnson at an auction of Confederate booty after the Civil War.

Considering the immense popularity of Ulysses Simpson Grant, it is somewhat surprising that so little remains in ceramic tributes to his heroic military victories. It is perhaps more fitting that the American glass-bottle makers used his image frequently on whiskey flasks, for Grant had a reputation for being a heavy drinker. His drinking problem caused him to be relieved of his army command and to resign his commission as captain in May 1854, but he was called back into the army by Lincoln in 1861. The rest of U. S. Grant's military career is history. When Lincoln was assassinated, Grant became the most popular man in the country, and it was obvious to President Johnson that Grant would be the Republican nominee in 1868. Johnson had withstood months of vituperative oration as Congress attempted to impeach him, and he had hoped for vindication by his party in the 1868 convention. However, it was not to come, and General Grant had no trouble beating the opposing candidate in the election, Horatio Seymour. Johnson did not attend Ulysses Grant's inauguration.

The alphabet plate in Figure 149 is probably a campaign item. It depicts a grim Major General Grant in military uniform.

Fig. 150 Small Parian bust of Grant. (DEWITT COLLECTION, UNIVERSITY OF HARTFORD. PHOTOGRAPH BY CHARLES KLAMKIN)

17

RUTHERFORD B. HAYES JAMES GARFIELD, AND CHESTER ARTHUR CHINA

Rutherford Birchard Hayes, nineteenth president of the United States, dedicated his administration to bringing a divided country together again. He had been instrumental in forming the Republican party in Ohio and was eventually elected to the office of city solicitor in Cincinnati. Hayes later lost that office and entered the army as a major after the attack on Fort Sumter. His army career was successful, and he rose to the rank of brigadier general. He was elected to Congress while still in the army and in 1867 was nominated for governor of Ohio on the Republican ticket. He won that election and held the office for two terms. He ran for Congress once more in 1872, but was defeated, and in 1875 he was again drafted by his party for a third term as governor. He won this time and then became mentioned as a possible candidate for the presidency. At the Republican convention it appeared that James G. Blaine would win the nomination, but Hayes won on the seventh ballot. His Democratic opponent was Samuel J. Tilden. Hayes's running mate was lawyer and banker William A. Wheeler.

Hayes did not campaign to any extent and was rarely seen in public during the months before election. He did attend the centennial celebration in Philadelphia, and the brown stoneware mug in Figure 153 probably dates from that occasion. Hayes was hardly an impressive figure in any case, and the small toby pitcher in Figure 151 is probably a rather accurate likeness of the short, rumpled, poorly dressed man. The intaglio tile (Figure 152) made in Hayes's home state of Ohio is somewhat more dignified and was undoubtedly made after the election.

120

PLATE 17

Left. *Blue printed souvenir plate of William McKinley's home.* (DEWITT COLLECTION, UNIVERSITY OF HARTFORD. PHOTOGRAPH BY CHARLES KLAMKIN)

Below. *Colorful plate shows portrait of William Jennings Bryan as a young man. Because of his lengthy career in politics, one can see him "age" on his own campaign plates.* (MR. AND MRS. LEON WEISSEL. PHOTOGRAPH BY CHARLES KLAMKIN)

Above. *William Jennings Bryan plate, probably made during his second or third try for the White House.* (DEWITT COLLECTION, UNIVERSITY OF HARTFORD. PHOTOGRAPH BY CHARLES KLAMKIN)

PLATE 18

Above. *Red, white, and blue bordered plate has polychrome printed portrait of Theodore Roosevelt.* (DEWITT COLLECTION, UNIVERSITY OF HARTFORD. PHOTOGRAPH BY CHARLES KLAMKIN)

Above. *Toby mug of "Rough Rider" Theodore Roosevelt depicts the president in his uniform and carrying gun and book.* (MR. AND MRS. LEON WEISSEL. PHOTOGRAPH BY CHARLES KLAMKIN)

Above. *Blue printed plate with portrait of Theodore Roosevelt and scenes from his life on the border.* (DEWITT COLLECTION, UNIVERSITY OF HARTFORD. PHOTOGRAPH BY CHARLES KLAMKIN)

PLATE 19

Above. *Clay pipe in configuration of head of Theodore Roosevelt.*
(SMITHSONIAN INSTITUTION PHOTOGRAPH)

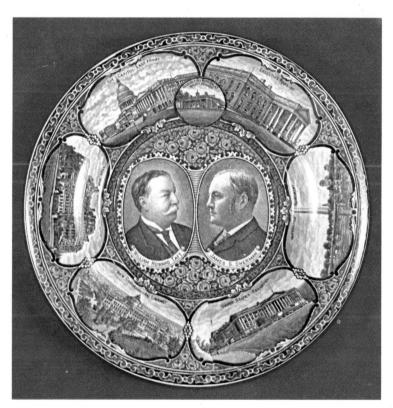

Above. *Taft-Sherman blue printed plate with scenes of Washington and
other places and high points of Taft's career.* (DEWITT COLLECTION,
UNIVERSITY OF HARTFORD. PHOTOGRAPH BY CHARLES KLAMKIN)

PLATE 20

Below. *Ceramic bust of William Howard Taft probably made during his presidency.* (DEWITT COLLECTION, UNIVERSITY OF HARTFORD. PHOTOGRAPH BY CHARLES KLAMKIN)

Above. *Taft campaign plate for 1908. Portrait printed in sepia.* (DEWITT COLLECTION, UNIVERSITY OF HARTFORD. PHOTOGRAPH BY CHARLES KLAMKIN)

Below. *Blue and white tile of Woodrow Wilson, an imitation of Wedgwood's jasperware. Made in 1916 by the Mosaic Tile Company in Zanesville, Ohio. A companion tile of Abraham Lincoln was made at the same time.* (DEWITT COLLECTION, UNIVERSITY OF HARTFORD. PHOTOGRAPHY BY CHARLES KLAMKIN)

Above. *"Smiling Bill and Sunny Jim" plate. Written in banner, "An Invincible Combination."* (DEWITT COLLECTION, UNIVERSITY OF HARTFORD. PHOTOGRAPH BY CHARLES KLAMKIN)

PLATE 21

Left. *Wedgwood Queen's Ware cup and saucer in "Liberty" pattern, designed and sold by an American to raise money for British war relief during World War I. Pattern was also made in bone china in different shape.* (AUTHOR'S COLLECTION. PHOTOGRAPH BY CHARLES KLAMKIN)

Below. *Plate with portrait of Woodrow Wilson shows how president aged through war and illness.* (MR. AND MRS. LEON WEISSEL. PHOTOGRAPH BY CHARLES KLAMKIN)

Below. *"Strange Bedfellows" pocket flask of blue glazed earthenware shows Bryan and Wilson snuggled together in cheerful coziness. This is one of the most interesting of all ceramic political relics.* (DEWITT COLLECTION, UNIVERSITY OF HARTFORD. PHOTOGRAPH BY CHARLES KLAMKIN)

PLATE 22

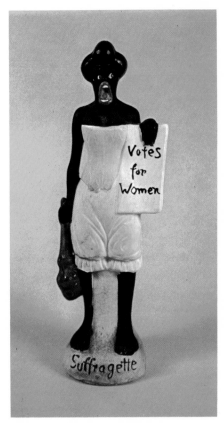

Above. *Black woman activist Sojourner Truth wore corsets in Suffragette parades, carried a club, and was very vociferous in fighting for votes for women at the turn of the century. This bisque statuette (height, 6 inches) illustrates women's efforts to get the vote.* (MR. AND MRS. LEON WEISSEL. PHOTOGRAPH BY CHARLES KLAMKIN)

Above. *While many women activists were fighting for the vote, Carry A. Nation's fight was against alcohol.* (MR. AND MRS. LEON WEISSEL. PHOTOGRAPH BY CHARLES KLAMKIN)

Above. *While Carry Nation and others fought against whiskey, others in the country were for it. This ceramic plaque, made around 1920, is a permanent record of the feelings of those who nostalgically remembered "The Good Old Days" before Prohibition.* (MR. AND MRS. LEON WEISSEL. PHOTOGRAPH BY CHARLES KLAMKIN)

PLATE 23

Above. *Minton souvenir vase celebrating the visit of King George VI and Queen Elizabeth to this country in 1939.* (AUTHOR'S COLLECTION. PHOTOGRAPH BY CHARLES KLAMKIN)

Below. *Reverse of Minton vase showing eagle with motto of trip, "Friendship Makes Peace," in shield.*

PLATE 24

Left. *Wartime plate showing portrait of Franklin D. Roosevelt surrounded by eagles and flags of Allies.* (DR. EDMUND SULLIVAN. PHOTOGRAPH BY CHARLES KLAMKIN)

Right. *Wedgwood blue printed plate with portrait of Franklin Delano Roosevelt.* (DEWITT COLLECTION, UNIVERSITY OF HARTFORD. PHOTOGRAPH BY CHARLES KLAMKIN)

PLATE 25

Left. *"For Democracy," wartime plate showing older Roosevelt with Churchill. Oncoming battleship and flags of both nations complete center medallion.*
(MR. AND MRS. LEON WEISSEL. PHOTOGRAPH BY CHARLES KLAMKIN)

Below. *Portrait plate of President Harry S Truman.*
(MR. AND MRS. LEON WEISSEL. PHOTOGRAPH OF CHARLES KLAMKIN)

Above. *Washington souvenir plate has portrait of President and Mrs. Dwight D. Eisenhower.*
(MR. AND MRS. LEON WEISSEL. PHOTOGRAPH BY CHARLES KLAMKIN)

PLATE 26

Above. *Wedgwood jasperware sweet dish with profile portrait of President Kennedy.* (AUTHOR'S COLLECTION. PHOTOGRAPH BY CHARLES KLAMKIN)

Above. *Campaign ashtray made for Senator Everett McKinley Dirkson of Illinois, a man who was part of the Washington scene for many years.* (MR. AND MRS. LEON WEISSEL. PHOTOGRAPH BY CHARLES KLAMKIN)

Above. *Multicolor print of eagle on plate made around 1920.* (DEWITT COLLECTION, UNIVERSITY OF HARTFORD. PHOTOGRAPH BY CHARLES KLAMKIN)

PLATE 27

Above. *American symbols, the eagle, flag, etc., have been used to adorn plates for two hundred years. This plate, ca. 1890, was printed, hand-painted, and potted in England.* (DEWITT COLLECTION, UNIVERSITY OF HARTFORD. PHOTOGRAPH BY CHARLES KLAMKIN)

Left. *A less partisan shaving mug has Old Glory as a decoration.* (DEWITT COLLECTION, UNIVERSITY OF HARTFORD. PHOTOGRAPH BY CHARLES KLAMKIN)

PLATE 28

Above. "*Our Martyred Heroes*" *became a popular theme among craftsmen after McKinley's death. This ceramic canteen with portraits of assassinated Presidents Lincoln, Garfield, and McKinley was probably sold in Washington, D. C., souvenir shops around 1902.* (DEWITT COLLECTION, UNIVERSITY OF HARTFORD. PHOTOGRAPH BY CHARLES KLAMKIN)

PLATE 29

Left. *Reverse of "Our Martyred Heroes" canteen has decoration of medal with colorful flag ribbon.* (DEWITT COLLECTION, UNIVERSITY OF HARTFORD. PHOTO BY CHARLES KLAMKIN)

Right. *The American flag decorates a porcelain candy dish that was probably made in France. Ribbon and laurel add proper Victorian touch.* (DEWITT COLLECTION, UNIVERSITY OF HARTFORD. PHOTOGRAPH BY CHARLES KLAMKIN)

PLATE 30

Right. "Our Martyred Heroes" plate with portraits of Lincoln, Garfield and McKinley surrounded by typical border from turn of the century. (DEWITT COLLECTION, UNIVERSITY OF HARTFORD. PHOTOGRAPH BY CHARLES KLAMKIN)

Right. Souvenir plate with portraits of presidents. This colorful platter with a picture of the White House was copyrighted in 1909. (MRS. MARJORIE HARDY. PHOTOGRAPH BY CHARLES KLAMKIN)

PLATE 31

Left. *Souvenir presidents' plate made during Truman administration.* (MR. AND MRS. LEON WEISSEL. PHOTOGRAPH BY CHARLES KLAMKIN)

Right. *By the time of John F. Kennedy's administration, thirty-five presidents crowded this printed plate.* (MR. AND MRS. LEON WEISSEL. PHOTO-GRAPH BY CHARLES KLAMKIN)

PLATE 32

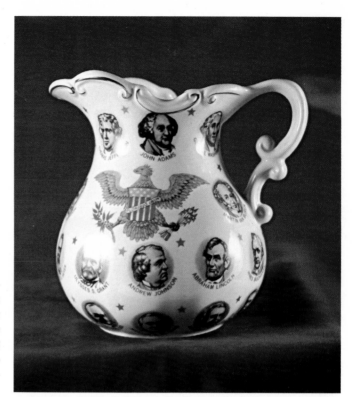

Right. *With too many presidents to fit on a plate by the time of Lyndon Johnson's administration, the Japanese printed this Victorian-looking pitcher instead.* (MR. AND MRS. LEON WEISSEL. PHOTOGRAPH BY CHARLES KLAMKIN)

Right. *Our thirty-sixth president, Lyndon Johnson, can be seen in bottom row on reverse of pitcher made in Japan. He is next to President Kennedy.* (MR. AND MRS. LEON WEISSEL. PHOTOGRAPH BY CHARLES KLAMKIN)

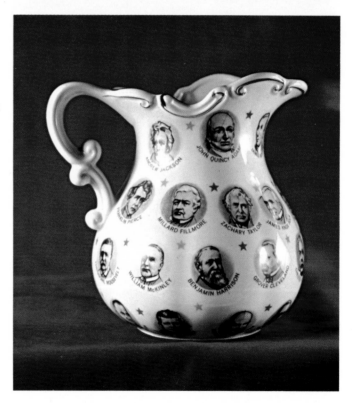

Fig. 151 Small ceramic figure of Rutherford B. Hayes. (MR. AND MRS. LEON WEISSEL. PHOTOGRAPH BY CHARLES KLAMKIN)

Fig. 152 Intaglio tile portrait of Rutherford Birchard Hayes. These portrait tiles were one of the finest accomplishments of American potters of the period. (MR. AND MRS. LEON WEISSEL. PHOTOGRAPH BY CHARLES KLAMKIN)

Fig. 153 Mug, redware with dark brown glaze, is souvenir of campaign of Hayes and running mate, William A. Wheeler. (DEWITT COLLECTION, UNIVERSITY OF HARTFORD. PHOTOGRAPH BY CHARLES KLAMKIN)

Fig. 154 Campaign plate for James A. Garfield in 1880. Garfield was shot by an assassin only four months after his election. (MR. AND MRS. LEON WEISSEL. PHOTOGRAPH BY CHARLES KLAMKIN)

Fig. 155 General Winfield Scott Hancock was Democratic candidate running against Garfield in 1880. (DEWITT COLLECTION, UNIVERSITY OF HARTFORD. PHOTOGRAPH BY CHARLES KLAMKIN)

Fig. 156 Chester A. Arthur became president after Garfield died. (MR. AND MRS. LEON WEISSEL. PHOTOGRAPH BY CHARLES KLAMKIN)

Fig. 157 This campaign plate, printed in black, plays up army careers of both candidates. Plate was made and printed in New Jersey, as was most campaign china of this period. (MATTATUCK MUSEUM. PHOTOGRAPH BY CHARLES KLAMKIN)

Although he did not actually seek nomination for president, it can be said that James Abram Garfield literally talked his way into office. He was an evangelist as well as a teacher and had a reputation for being a great orator and debater. Garfield started life as the son of a poor farmer from Ohio and worked his way through college, at first attending Western Reserve Eclectic Institute and then finishing at Williams College in Williamstown, Massachusetts. Garfield returned to Ohio with his eastern diploma and was appointed president of his first alma mater, the name of which had been changed to Hiram College. By the spring of 1859 Garfield had run successfully for the office of state senator in Ohio.

Garfield served in the Civil War and rose to the rank of brigadier general. In 1862, while Garfield was still on the field of battle, the Republican party in Ohio chose him as a candidate for the House of Representatives. After he had been elected to Congress, he returned to the battlefield to finish his more important political battle, and it was now his ambition to become senator from Ohio. However, he was instrumental in aiding in the election of Rutherford B. Hayes, and Hayes had requested that Garfield remain in the House of Representatives. By 1880 Garfield felt that he deserved to be a senator, and he was elected. He had served as congressman for eighteen years, and his record was unblemished. He was well known nationally.

It was a peculiar combination of circumstances that caused Garfield to be elected to the Senate and the presidency in the same year. In 1880 the Republican party was divided into two factions, the Stalwarts and the Half-Breeds. It was the Stalwarts' ambition to renominate former president U. S. Grant. The Half-Breeds' candidate was James G. Blaine. Other candidates' names were also mentioned and given votes on the earlier balloting. John Sherman's name was put up to the convention by Garfield, whose gift for oratory was, by this time, well known and appreciated. On the second day of balloting, Sherman requested that his votes be thrown to Garfield, and he received seventeen votes on the thirty-fourth ballot. Garfield modestly protested that no one had a right to announce a candidate's name without his consent. Two ballots later, Garfield was the Republican presidential candidate. He was never to sit in the Senate.

Garfield's opponent during the campaign was Winfield Scott Hancock, a man with an untarnished record and a rather bland personality. Issues were difficult for either party to find during the campaign. Therefore, as often happens, the campaign was brought to the rather low level of personalities. There, too, it was difficult to find scandalous material for campaign invective, and Hancock was narrowly defeated by Garfield. Several months after the election, on July 2, 1881, Hancock could not have been too unhappy about not having achieved the highest office in the land. On that day Garfield was shot by a disappointed office seeker, Charles J. Guiteau. It took Garfield's well-meaning physicians two and a half months to finish the job, thereby making Chester Alan Arthur president of the United States.

Because Garfield had only four short months as president of the United States, it is probable that all Garfield-related pottery and porcelain are either campaign objects or memorials to Garfield following his death. The Wedgwood creamware pitcher (see Plate 12) is a memorial to Garfield, but it has none of the symbols of death usually found on late-Victorian pottery of a commemorative nature. Most certainly the Garfield plates (see Plate 13) are campaign plates, since they match perfectly those showing the face of Garfield's opponent, Winfield Hancock. Pottery of a memorial nature with Garfield's image can be found on the several

Fig. 158 Garfield stoneware pitcher with raised and hand-painted decoration was probably made following the death of the president. (DEWITT COLLECTION, UNIVERSITY OF HARTFORD. PHOTOGRAPH BY CHARLES KLAMKIN)

items that contain portraits of "Our Martyred Heroes," which, when made, numbered only three presidents.

The first public office Chester Arthur was to obtain was that of vice president under Garfield. His experience in politics had been confined to chairmanship of the New York Republican Executive Committee, under Grant, and in 1871 Grant had appointed Arthur, a successful New York attorney, to take charge of the New York Customs House. Grant needed Arthur's reputation for honesty to help dispel the stories of scandals about his first appointee, Thomas Murphy. The Customs House provided 1,000 party workers with patronage through many elections, and Arthur held the position until 1877.

Arthur, like Garfield, was a compromise candidate for the office of vice president. However, after the lengthy battle at that convention for the presidency, Arthur was given second place on the first ballot. He stated at the time he was nominated that the vice presidency was a higher office than he had ever dreamed of attaining, and, therefore, he considered the nomination a great honor. His party obviously did not feel the same way about him. He was a scrupulously honest man, but his name had erroneously been linked with scandals connected to the New York Customs House, and little else could be said either against or for him.

Garfield's assassin, Charles Guiteau, did not make accession to the White House easier for Arthur. Guiteau claimed he had shot the president in order to make Chester Arthur president. The country had eleven weeks to get used to the idea of Arthur becoming president of the United States. While Garfield was lingering near death Arthur remained in New York, ignoring those who thought of his assuming the presidency as a tragedy.

When election time came around again, the Republican party was still split, and Chester Arthur, who had been, after all, a passable president, was unable to get support for a nomination in his own right. Therefore, any Arthur mementos can be dated to 1880, the year Garfield was nominated for president and Arthur was chosen as his running mate.

18

GROVER CLEVELAND AND BENJAMIN HARRISON CHINA

Portly Grover Cleveland is our only president to have staged a comeback after having been in office one term and losing the next election. His first term in the White House began in 1885, and he lost the next election to Benjamin Harrison by an electoral vote of 223 to 168. Cleveland had Thomas A. Hendricks as his running mate for his 1885 election. Hendricks was from Indiana and was placed on the ticket to strengthen the party in the Midwest. He lived only a few months after his election, and during Cleveland's first term he did not have a vice president.

In his attempt to regain his position in the White House, Cleveland had chosen as a running mate Allen Granberry Thurman. Thurman was fated never to have the job he sought, and Adlai E. Stevenson served under Cleveland when he finally returned to the White House in 1893. Interestingly, Stevenson ran again for vice president on the Democratic ticket, headed by William Jennings Bryan, in 1900.

Although a few different campaign plates remain from the Cleveland era, the majority of those that do exist were made for the one campaign that Cleveland lost. A stern-looking Cleveland is touted "For President" on several campaign plates, and on others he is joined by an equally stern-looking Thurman. The plate shape for the 1888 campaign, which bears likenesses of both candidates and has the embossed legend in the border "Give us this day/Our daily bread," was originally designed and made by Isaac Davis of Trenton, New Jersey, for

Fig. 159 Grover Cleveland campaign plate. Made for first campaign in 1884. (SMITHSONIAN INSTITUTION PHOTOGRAPH)

Fig. 160 Thomas A. Hendricks was Cleveland's running mate, but his term as vice president was cut short when he died in November 1885. (DEWITT COLLECTION, UNIVERSITY OF HARTFORD. PHOTOGRAPH BY CHARLES KLAMKIN)

Fig. 161 James G. Blaine was Cleveland's opponent in 1884. (DEWITT COLLECTION, UNIVERSITY OF HARTFORD. PHOTOGRAPH BY CHARLES KLAMKIN)

Fig. 162 Benjamin Harrison campaign plate. Made in 1888. (MR. AND MRS. LEON WEISSEL. PHOTOGRAPH BY CHARLES KLAMKIN)

127

Fig. 163 Campaign plate printed with Benjamin Harrison's portrait was made in New Jersey. (SMITHSONIAN INSTITUTION PHOTOGRAPH)

Fig. 164 Vice presidential candidate in 1888 for Republican party was Levi P. Morton. (SMITHSONIAN INSTITUTION PHOTOGRAPH)

the centennial celebration in 1876. Its original design had a view of Horticultural Hall, Centennial Building, in the center.

Cleveland's second successful try for the presidency was the prelude to four difficult years in the White House. Against much strong opposition he was able to maintain the gold standard and he recalled a treaty drawn up during Harrison's administration to annex Hawaii, but he also made many mistakes in managing the labor disputes that plagued his last years as president. William Jennings Bryan won the Democratic nomination for president with his famous "Cross of Gold" speech.

Benjamin Harrison, the president whose term was sandwiched in between Cleveland's two terms, was elected through a combination of corruption and the Republican party. National Republican Committee Chairman Matt Quay had bought votes and bribed and threatened to put the colorless Harrison into the White House. In 1888 even the grandson of a former president needed the Quay touch to get elected.

James G. Blaine, head of the Republican party in 1888, declared early that he would not be a candidate for office, and Harrison was Blaine's choice. He was nominated on the eighth ballot, and Levi P. Morton was his choice for vice president. Bearded Benjamin Harrison is the subject of several campaign plates. Levi P. Morton is shown as well on some matching campaign plates.

Fig. 165 *Grover Cleveland ran with Allan G. Thurman against Benjamin Harrison in 1888.* *White china pin tray was campaign item.* (DR. EDMUND SULLIVAN. PHOTOGRAPH BY CHARLES KLAMKIN)

Fig. 166 *Cleveland-Thurman bread plate was centennial design made in New Jersey. Twelve years later the same mold was used for campaign plate.* (MR. AND MRS. LEON WEISSEL. PHOTOGRAPH BY CHARLES KLAMKIN)

James G. Blaine, the candidate for the Republican party who ran against Grover Cleveland in 1884, was a man whose god was money. He had been the son of a family that had once had money and power but had lost it before Blaine was born. Blaine spent the rest of his life attempting to recover what he must have felt was his birthright. The manner in which Blaine got his fortune was the cause for his losing the presidency.

Blaine was elected to Congress from the state of Maine and served almost twenty years as representative, speaker of the house, and senator. He had wanted the nomination in 1876 and in 1880, but his opponents charged that he had shady dealings with the railroads while serving as speaker of the house. There is no indication that the charges against Blaine were anything but accurate. However, there is also no indication that Blaine was ever convinced that it was wrong to receive money or support from the railroad interests while serving as an elected official.

The political campaigns of 1884 have been described as "low level." Issues were less important than muckraking, and Cleveland answered his adversary's story that Cleveland had an illegitimate son with cries of "liar, cheat, crook and hypocrite." Blaine's party members had equivalent epithets for Cleveland. The campaign was so low that even Blaine's wife came in for the same sort of criticism that had been so harmful to Rachel and Andrew Jackson. It was rumored that the Blaine marriage was in doubt since the marriage ceremony had first been performed in secret and then was followed by a second, more public, ceremony a few months later. A child born to the Blaines had died in infancy, and it was asserted that this child, long gone and possibly forgotten, had been illegitimate. The opposition carried on in the same vein by charging Grover Cleveland with the fathering of an illegitimate child of his own. The statesmanlike portraits on the late-nineteenth-century campaign plates depicting Blaine and Cleveland belie the quality of the 1884 campaign, in which Blaine lost to Cleveland by very few votes.

19

DESIGNS RELATING TO WILLIAM McKINLEY AND WILLIAM JENNINGS BRYAN

William McKinley, twenty-fifth president of the United States, is the subject of many souvenir and campaign plates. He is also included on pottery or porcelain decorated to honor our martyred presidents. A popular Republican congressman with a record of rapid success in soldiering during the Civil War, McKinley was an attractive, well-liked man. However, there are other reasons for the abundance of McKinley campaign materials for collectors.

A strong advocate of protective tariff laws, McKinley was instrumental in passing the historic tariff bill while still in Congress. He lost his seat in Congress during the campaign in which Benjamn Harrison was elected president (in 1890), but he drew the attention of Mark Hanna, a wealthy Cleveland businessman who had a great deal of political power. With Hanna's help and backing, McKinley was elected governor of Ohio in 1891 and was reelected to that office in 1893. Important business interests, as well as Mr. Hanna, were soundly behind McKinley when he was nominated for president in 1896, against William Jennings Bryan. Bryan advocated the free coinage of silver, while McKinley wanted to place America on the gold standard, a measure that was finally adopted in 1900.

William McKinley made all of his carefully written campaign speeches from the porch of his house in Canton, Ohio, and he and his running mate, Garret A. Hobart, won the election. Plates that bear both Hobart and McKinley's images

Fig. 167 Intaglio tiles of candidates William McKinley and Garret A. Hobart. Used as campaign items. Reverse has printed biographies of candidates. Made in 1896 by American Encaustic Tiling Co. Ltd., Zanesville, Ohio. (DEWITT COLLECTION, UNIVERSITY OF HARTFORD. PHOTOGRAPH BY CHARLES KLAMKIN)

Fig. 168 Campaign tile with portrait of McKinley. (DEWITT COLLECTION, UNIVERSITY OF HARTFORD. PHOTOGRAPH BY CHARLES KLAMKIN)

Fig. 169 In 1896 the candidates of the Republican party were William McKinley and Garret A. Hobart. The team had almost unlimited financial backing, and there were a great many campaign items made for them. (DEWITT COLLECTION, UNIVERSITY OF HARTFORD. PHOTOGRAPH BY CHARLES KLAMKIN)

are, of course, from this campaign. Money was no object, since Mark Hanna had been able to raise hitherto unheard-of sums for the McKinley-Hobart campaign. Furthermore, the business interests supporting McKinley felt it unnecessary (and possibly damaging) for the candidate to bring his message directly to the people, and the possibility of bringing the presidential hopeful's likeness to the public through the distribution of portrait plates seemed an excellent idea. A great many plates were printed with McKinley's portrait. He was handsome, beardless, and clean-cut, and few members of his party were not acquainted with McKinley's countenance by election time.

Any president who has been able to improve the economy of the country is bound to gain in popularity, and such was the case with McKinley. Backed by the strong power of big business and sponsored by Mark Hanna's enormous wealth and drive, McKinley, with Theodore Roosevelt as his vice presidential candidate, ran successfully for a second time against William Jennings Bryan. The Spanish-American War had been fought during McKinley's first administration, and Bryan charged that the United States was becoming an imperialist nation. However, McKinley had run on a "full dinner pail" platform, and this again won him the election.

By the time McKinley ran for president in 1889, the era of large campaign funds and the resultant ballyhoo that goes with American presidential campaigns had already become a tradition. With Hanna's money and other large sums from Republican supporters, a great many campaign souvenirs were again manufactured and circulated. The astronomical sum for the time of 3 1/2 million dollars was raised by the Republicans for the first McKinley campaign, while the Democrats fought back with only 1 million dollars.

Since the issue of free silver was uppermost during McKinley's first campaign, William Jennings Bryan in his famous "Cross of Gold" speech declared, "You shall not press down upon the brow of labor this crown of thorns; you shall not crucify mankind upon a cross of gold." Bryan's party became known as the Gold Bugs, with the opposition's issue used against Bryan's party in much the way that the log cabin issue had been used to help William Henry Harrison. Thousands of souvenirs carried the gold bug theme to the people. One interesting nonceramic souvenir of that election is a small gold bug whose wings unfurl to reveal photographs of McKinley and Hobart. Many plates were also printed with portraits of the two candidates or with just McKinley's handsome image on them.

Fig. 170 Above *McKinley tile printed in polychrome. Mark Hanna saw to it that McKinley's face would be recognized across the country, but kept the candidate at home on his front porch throughout the campaign.* (MR. AND MRS. LEON WEISSEL. PHOTOGRAPH BY CHARLES KLAMKIN)

Fig. 171 Right *Small china pin tray showing birthplace of William McKinley.* (DR. EDMUND SULLIVAN. PHOTOGRAPH BY CHARLES KLAMKIN)

Fig. 172 *Small Parian bust of William McKinley.* (DEWITT COLLECTION, UNIVERSITY OF HARTFORD. PHOTOGRAPH BY CHARLES KLAMKIN)

Fig. 173 *In 1901 McKinley was shot by anarchist Leon Czolgosz. This plate is memorial to another martyred president.* (MR. AND MRS. LEON WEISSEL. PHOTOGRAPH BY CHARLES KLAMKIN)

In proof that the party which spends the most money can often win an election, McKinley won by a large margin in his first campaign for the presidency. He and Hobart did well too. McKinley received 271 electoral votes to Bryan's 176.

Interestingly, while campaign slogans and promises, as well as slurs against the opposing party, are all part of American political campaigns and show up time after time on many more ephemeral campaign items than china, there seems to be some idea in the minds of those who order campaign items that plates are not a suitable medium for promises that might come back to haunt the candidate if he is elected. It is understood that pottery and porcelain items are usually more lasting than posters, campaign toys, bandannas, and buttons. In his management of McKinley's campaign, Mark Hanna seemed to understand this fact. The use of color lithography for inexpensive plate decoration led to the ordering of a great many plates with colorful borders and the rosy-complexioned McKinley smiling in the center.

Not only the presidential winners and their running mates have been subjects of plate decoration. One can also find plates with the noble features of many of the presidential losers. Some of these men are recognizable for activities other than just having lost an election, since they often played other important roles in American history. Such a man was William Jennings Bryan, the politician-

Fig. 174 The gold or silver issue was a strong one throughout the McKinley era, and this mug was made in celebration of McKinley victory over silver advocate William Jennings Bryan. (MR. AND MRS. LEON WEISSEL. PHOTOGRAPH BY CHARLES KLAMKIN)

Fig. 175 Two-handled campaign mug made for election of 1896. Arthur Sewell of Maine was the vice presidential candidate. (SMITHSONIAN INSTITUTION PHOTOGRAPH)

Fig. 176 William Jennings Bryan, on what was to be the first of many campaign items made for this perennial also-ran. (SMITHSONIAN INSTITUTION PHOTOGRAPH)

revivalist who ran for the office of president of the United States and lost three times.

Bryan was a product of midwestern morality. Following his failure to establish a law practice in his home state of Illinois, Bryan moved to Nebraska, where he would have less competition. During his clientless years he studied the history of the Democratic party and politics in general. He was a talented speaker and soon became known for his "silver tongue" and pious opinions concerning the value of man and the virtues of God. When he was elected to Congress in 1890, he was only thirty years old.

A religious fanatic, Bryan became so enamored of himself and his powers as a speaker who could move throngs to near-hysteria that he was convinced he was divinely ordained to lead the country. He loved seeing his picture in the newspapers and must have adored the campaign plates printed with his handsome features. His Democratic nomination for president in 1896 further convinced him that "God is me; I am God." As Irving Stone remarked in his book *They Also Ran*, "He had gone Hollywood."

Bryan was able to keep a strong hold on the Democratic party, and following his first defeat to McKinley in a very close vote he lectured and wrote until the next Democratic convention, when he was once again nominated. Again he lost.

136

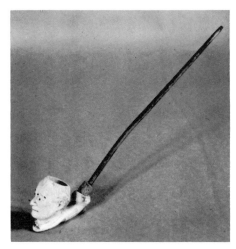

Fig. 177 William Jennings Bryan clay pipe was probably campaign give-away. (SMITHSONIAN INSTITUTION PHOTOGRAPH)

Fig. 178 William Jennings Bryan campaigned against McKinley in 1896 and again in 1900. This intaglio tile shows Bryan as he probably looked during first campaign. Tile made in Ohio. (MR. AND MRS. LEON WEISSEL. PHOTOGRAPH BY CHARLES KLAMKIN)

Fig. 179 Two china pin trays with prints of the Democratic candidates of 1896. Bryan and Hobart lost to McKinley. (MR. AND MRS. LEON WEISSEL. PHOTOGRAPH BY CHARLES KLAMKIN)

Fig. 180 Bryan, literally a "silver-throated orator," held the leadership of the Democratic party until Woodrow Wilson's time. China plate with printed portrait. (MR. AND MRS. LEON WEISSEL. PHOTOGRAPH BY CHARLES KLAMKIN)

Fig. 181 One of the most interesting political ceramic items is this brown-glazed American-made cup and saucer. Written in slip on saucer, "William J. Bryan, 1908." Medallion in white clay is impressed in cup. Note handle is Bryan's initials. (MR. AND MRS. LEON WEISSEL. PHOTOGRAPH BY CHARLES KLAMKIN)

There is little question that the superior man became president, but McKinley would have been hard to defeat in any case, with Mark Hanna as business manager of the Republican party. Millions were raised and spent on both of McKinley's campaigns for the presidency. While McKinley sat on his front porch in Ohio, Hanna's men were out buying votes in any manner possible. It is no coincidence that so many plates and other ceramic objects can be found with McKinley's or Bryan's portraits. The campaigns were competitive on a plate scale as well as a political one.

In the three elections in which Bryan was a candidate, the right men were elected by the wrong methods and probably for the wrong reasons. By the time Bryan lost his last election, in 1908, he had become an anachronism. He did not give up trying, however. In 1924 he ran for the nomination on an anti-evolution platform, and, having lost, spent the remainder of his life fighting to have the teaching of science banned in the public schools.

Figure 181 is a Bryan campaign item made during his 1908 attempt to capture the Democratic nomination. The pocket flask in Plate 21 is an interesting ceramic relic of Bryan's later career in politics (see Chapter 20).

20

DESIGNS RELATING TO THEODORE ROOSEVELT, WILLIAM HOWARD TAFT, AND WOODROW WILSON

Theodore Roosevelt was a natural for the plate makers at the beginning of this century. His fame as a member of the Rough Riders and his legendary refusal to shoot a bear cub while on a hunting trip gave rise to many imaginative toby pitchers and ceramic toys. Roosevelt, of course, became president following McKinley's death by assassination. His popularity, however, carried him through another full term and won him the next election on his own merits.

Roosevelt did not especially want to run for the office of vice president in 1896, nor did McKinley want him as a running mate. However, his nomination was a way to get him removed from politics in New York. Roosevelt, an honest man, had bucked the political machine in his state too often as governor. While McKinley serenely campaigned from his front porch, Roosevelt waged a colorful and energetic campaign and made many friends.

Young and exuberant, Roosevelt inspired the manufacture of many objects that are representative of events that occurred during his eight years in office. Of particular interest is the plate in Figure 186. Called "Digging the Ditch at Panama," the decoration shows industrious "Teddy bears" with shovels. A verse accompanies the picture:

> *To finish this great work*
> *We need no foreign aid.*
> *For we can do it all ourselves*
> *With spirit and with spade.*

Fig. 182 Theodore Roosevelt seemed to inspire more than a few toby mugs and pitchers. This one uses his gun for a handle and is not a caricature, as many toby mugs and pitchers were. (MR. AND MRS. LEON WEISSEL. PHOTOGRAPH BY CHARLES KLAMKIN)

Fig. 183 A rather glum Theodore Roosevelt adorns this souvenir mug. (MR. AND MRS. LEON WEISSEL. PHOTOGRAPH BY CHARLES KLAMKIN)

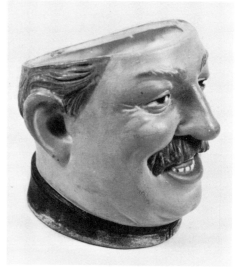

Fig. 184 Intaglio glazed portrait tile of Theodore Roosevelt with its own frame. (MR. AND MRS. LEON WEISSEL. PHOTOGRAPH BY CHARLES KLAMKIN)

Fig. 185 Theodore Roosevelt's large white teeth were almost considered a trade mark. This pottery jar (lid missing) shows a smiling, open-mouthed president. (MR. AND MRS. LEON WEISSEL. PHOTOGRAPH BY CHARLES KLAMKIN)

Fig. 186 Teddy bears were used as motifs on many Roosevelt items. These bears are shown "Digging the Ditch at Panama." Polychrome print. (MR. AND MRS. LEON WEISSEL. PHOTOGRAPH BY CHARLES KLAMKIN)

Fig. 187 China pitcher showing teacher bear attempting to control unruly baby bears. (MR. AND MRS. LEON WEISSEL. PHOTOGRAPH BY CHARLES KLAMKIN)

Fig. 188 "Five million votes in the bag" and "Teddy and the Bear." Roosevelt campaign china items. Roosevelt disliked nickname "Teddy," and his friends never used it. (MR. AND MRS. LEON WEISSEL. PHOTOGRAPH BY CHARLES KLAMKIN)

The plate is a commemorative of Roosevelt's efforts to convince Congress that the United States should build a canal across Panama, which was then a part of Colombia. A French company, the New Panama Canal Company, owned the rights to the proposed canal through a previous agreement. Colombia at first agreed to the terms laid down by the United States, but later on backed down and demanded more money. On November 3, 1903, Panama, in a bloodless coup, declared its independence from Colombia, and shortly afterward the United States recognized Panama as an independent country. Roosevelt probably could not have foreseen the problems that would arise from this obviously

Fig. 189 More miniature china Teddy toys inspired by Theodore Roosevelt's presidency. (MR. AND MRS. LEON WEISSEL. PHOTOGRAPH BY CHARLES KLAMKIN)

Fig. 190 Presidential plate printed in dark blue and made by Wedgwood. (AUTHOR'S COLLECTION. PHOTOGRAPH BY CHARLES KLAMKIN)

Fig. 191 Memorial tile made following the death of Theodore Roosevelt. Printed photographic portrait. (MR. AND MRS. LEON WEISSEL. PHOTOGRAPH BY CHARLES KLAMKIN)

Fig. 192 Intaglio tile portrait of William Howard Taft. Black glaze makes it look like a photograph. (MR. AND MRS. LEON WEISSEL. PHOTOGRAPH BY CHARLES KLAMKIN)

Fig. 193 Taft-Sherman plate bordered in red and blue, with motifs of flag, eagle, and shield. (DEWITT COLLECTION, UNIVERSITY OF HARTFORD. PHOTOGRAPH BY CHARLES KLAMKIN)

Fig. 194 A rotund, affable Taft appears on this bone china plate. (DEWITT COLLECTION, UNIVERSITY OF HARTFORD. PHOTOGRAPH BY CHARLES KLAMKIN)

Fig. 195 An entire series of "Smiling Bill and Sunny Jim" plates was issued. This one is entitled "The Morning After." (DEWITT COLLECTION, UNIVERSITY OF HARTFORD. PHOTOGRAPH BY CHARLES KLAMKIN)

144

engineered revolution. He wanted the canal built and he got it. The interesting advertising plate (given away by a California shoe store) in Figure 210 has a print in the center showing a map of the finished canal. On a red, white, and blue border surrounding the map are portraits of every American president up to Woodrow Wilson. The plate celebrates the completion of the canal in 1915.

For the majority of Americans, T. R., as he was known, could do no wrong, and he was nominated by his party on the first ballot in 1904. Charles Warren Fairbanks was chosen as his running mate. Alton B. Parker was the choice for presidential candidate of the Democratic party. It was generally conceded that Roosevelt would win by a landslide in any case. Even William Jennings Bryan knew enough not to run this time.

No president until Theodore Roosevelt was so outgoing and showmanlike. However, after William Howard Taft became president, it was obvious that Roosevelt could not abide taking second place to anyone, even a close friend. In 1912 Roosevelt ran for office on a third-party ticket and was defeated by Woodrow Wilson.

If presidents of the United States were elected by the pound, the American people would have had an enormous bargain in William Howard Taft. Taft's dimpled, mustached face can be found on souvenir plates from his two successive political campaigns for the presidency. The campaign plates were successful aids in Taft's first campaign. When he received his party's nomination again in 1912, no campaign plates would have helped. Taft's old friend turned enemy, Theodore Roosevelt, formed a third party and helped defeat Taft and elect Wilson.

Taft, a Cincinnati lawyer, judge, politician, and diplomat, had been a close friend of Theodore Roosevelt and was active in several capacities during the latter's administration. First, he served as governor of the Philippines and later as Roosevelt's secretary of war. As Roosevelt's friend and protégé Taft was promoted by the president for nomination at the Republican convention in 1908. Taft won the election from three-time loser William Jennings Bryan by more than a million votes.

As a balance for the Roosevelt candidate, and in resentment for not having had more to say about choosing their candidate, the delegates to the convention of 1908 chose an ultraconservative from New York, James S. Sherman, as Taft's running mate. The somewhat incongruous team has been immortalized on a series of cartoonlike plates issued after the election depicting "Smiling Bill and Sunny Jim" (see Plate 20 and Figure 4). The two are facing each other with wide

Fig. 196 Campaign plate for William Howard Taft, made in 1908.
(MR. AND MRS. LEON WEISSEL. PHOTOGRAPH BY CHARLES KLAMKIN)

Fig. 197 Campaign item with cartoon-type image of Taft and legend "A match for anyone." Item is a match striker. (DEWITT COLLECTION, UNIVERSITY OF HARTFORD. PHOTOGRAPH BY CHARLES KLAMKIN)

grins and "An Invincible Combination" is written on a banner between them. In truth, the relationship between these two men became difficult during their term in office, when Taft, caught between his friend Theodore Roosevelt, and his vice president, Sherman, in a New York political battle, sided with Roosevelt after having first favored Sherman. Sherman was nominated to run with Taft a second time, nevertheless, but died a week before the election.

Taft's second campaign was doomed by more than just the loss of his vice presidential candidate. Roosevelt's formation of the Progressive party gave Wilson the election. Taft, in 1921, finally got the job he really had wanted in the first place. In that year President Harding appointed him as chief justice of the Supreme Court. He remained head of the court for nine years.

Woodrow Wilson came to the Democratic convention in 1912 with a record as a successful teacher and writer, and a middle-of-the-road philosophy concerning the manner in which the country should be run. His political experience, however, was somewhat limited. He had spent two years as governor of New

146

Fig. 198 Toby mug of William Howard Taft. Same shape was made in several different clay bodies and glazes. This one is glazed in soft pastel colors. (MR. AND MRS. LEON WEISSEL. PHOTOGRAPH BY CHARLES KLAMKIN)

Fig. 199 Profile portrait of Taft. Ceramic plaque made of white clay and left unglazed. American. (DEWITT COLLECTION, UNIVERSITY OF HARTFORD. PHOTOGRAPH BY CHARLES KLAMKIN)

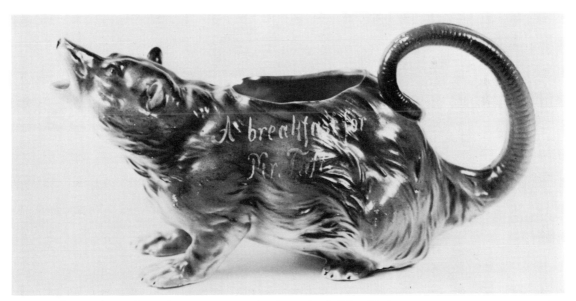

Fig. 200 China pitcher in shape of a possum was used as favor at a Taft breakfast. (MR. AND MRS. LEON WEISSELL. PHOTOGRAPH BY CHARLES KLAMKIN)

Jersey, and his first year had been brilliant enough to draw attention to the fact that he might be a good choice as a candidate for president. Wilson was no shoe-in for the nomination, however. He was finally nominated on the forty-sixth ballot. His Republican opponent was William Howard Taft. Theodore Roosevelt had defected from his party and was running on the Progressive or "Bull Moose" ticket. Eugene Debs was the Socialists' candidate.

Wilson waged a vigorous campaign that took him across the country, and he used the rear platform of the train as an actor would a stage. Taft, the incumbent, did very little active campaigning, and Roosevelt had lost much of his energy by 1912. After the long occupancy in the White House, the American people had obviously decided that it was time for a change, and Wilson won the election with 435 electoral votes. He received over two million more popular votes than Theodore Roosevelt and almost three million more than Taft. Taft, who had not wanted the presidency in the first place, left the White House to become Kent professor of constitutional law at Yale.

There are few pottery or porcelain relics that can be traced to the Wilson campaigns. However, one Wilson-related object (Plate 21) tells us some-

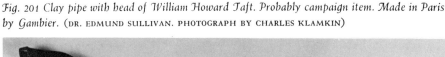

Fig. 201 Clay pipe with head of William Howard Taft. Probably campaign item. Made in Paris by Gambier. (DR. EDMUND SULLIVAN. PHOTOGRAPH BY CHARLES KLAMKIN)

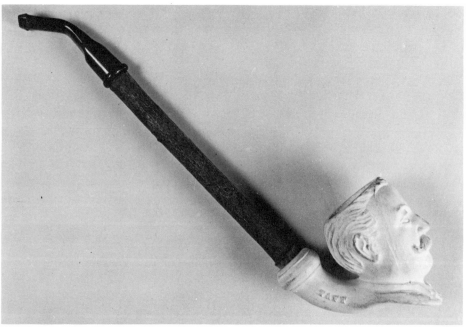

Fig. 202 Left *China pin tray with portrait of Taft was souvenir item from Syracuse, New York.* (DEWITT COLLECTION, UNIVERSITY OF HARTFORD. PHOTOGRAPH BY CHARLES KLAMKIN)

Fig. 203 Below *Match striker was probably campaign item during Woodrow Wilson's fight for the presidency in 1912.* (MR. AND MRS. LEON WEISSEL. PHOTOGRAPH BY CHARLES KLAMKIN)

Fig. 204 Right *Unlike many Wedgwood imitations made during this period, the Wilson and Lincoln tiles are clearly marked on the reverse.* (DEWITT COLLECTION, UNIVERSITY OF HARTFORD. PHOTOGRAPH BY CHARLES KLAMKIN)

thing about the political history of the 1912 Democratic convention. This is a small hip flask in the shape of a crib, and it shows Woodrow Wilson snuggling under the blanket with William Jennings Bryan. As mentioned, Bryan was, by 1912, a threetime loser as presidential nominee of the Democratic party. However, he still had some strength and influence in his party. On the fourteenth ballot Bryan threw his votes to Wilson. Although it took many more votes than Bryan could gather for Wilson to be claimed the official candidate of that convention, it was obvious that Wilson owed the aging orator a debt, and after Wilson's election Bryan was appointed secretary of state.

The Wilson-Bryan relationship went back to the convention of 1908, when, following Bryan's nomination, Wilson had refused to share a speaker's platform with him. In 1912 Bryan was, of course, much more broadminded than Wilson had been. The whiskey flask, showing the two Democrats in cozy proximity, is, therefore, a potter's expression of that old maxim "Politics make strange bedfellows!"

Fig. 205 *Portrait plate of Wilson was souvenir item from Camp Dix, New Jersey, during World War I.* (MR. AND MRS. LEON WEISSEL. PHOTOGRAPH BY CHARLES KLAMKIN)

Fig. 206 *Black glazed portrait intaglio tile of Woodrow Wilson.* (MR. AND MRS. DAVID J. FREINT. PHOTOGRAPH BY CHARLES KLAMKIN)

If the extrovert Theodore Roosevelt and the smiling, rotund William Howard Taft both inspired plate manufacturers to make innovative campaign materials, Warren Gamaliel Harding, a man whose only real qualification for the presidency was that he looked the part, did not seem to inspire much in the way of ceramic memorials. His wife, Florence Kling DeWolfe Harding, was much more ambitious for the honor of having her husband elected president of the United States than he was. Harding had been happier as a senator, where he felt little pressure and could indulge almost full time his passion for card playing.

There were not enough campaign funds for the Harding faction to have campaign plates made. In addition, Harding was not allowed to travel throughout the campaign, but was kept at home in Ohio, where he was not even allowed to make any speeches. Harding's opponent was another Ohioan, James M. Cox, whose major claim to a place in American history is that he chose a young secretary of the navy, Franklin Delano Roosevelt, as his running mate. Harding beat the Democratic team by seven million votes. Calvin Coolidge was his vice president.

21

WOMEN'S SUFFRAGE, CALVIN COOLIDGE, HERBERT HOOVER, AND AL SMITH CHINA

There are a few ceramic relics that represent the first organized movement for women's suffrage in the United States. Causes as well as symbols and patriots have often been expressed on pottery and porcelain. In 1869 the National Woman Suffrage Association was founded by Susan B. Anthony and Elizabeth Cady Stanton. Its purpose was to work for a women's suffrage amendment to the Constitution. Others formed a separate organization to work for women's rights at a state level, and in 1890 the two organizations merged to become the National American Woman Suffrage Association.

The territorial legislature of Wyoming was the first to grant women the right to vote in 1869 and other western territories followed suit.

In the early twentieth century women who were working for the cause of suffrage had marched and demonstrated and had won the right to vote in thirty states by 1917. The nineteenth amendment to the Constitution was finally ratified in 1920.

Mrs. Belva Ann Bennett Lockwood was the presidential candidate of the National Equal Rights party in 1884 and 1888. She was the first woman attorney to plead before the Supreme Court, but she was not taken too seriously in some circles because she attempted to draw attention to her cause by riding a three-wheeled cycle through Washington streets wearing bright red stockings. It is highly probable that following one of her trips through the city she returned

Fig. 207 *China teacup and saucer with gold rim have suffrage slogan printed into discreet decoration.* (MR. AND MRS. LEON WEISSEL. PHOTOGRAPH BY CHARLES KLAMKIN)

Fig. 208 *The campaign for women's suffrage went on through many administrations. Most of the pottery and porcelain items having to do with the issue show too much restraint.* (DEWITT COLLECTION, UNIVERSITY OF HARTFORD. PHOTOGRAPH BY CHARLES KLAMKIN)

Fig. 209 *Small glazed pottery kitten pleads for "Votes for Women."* (MR. AND MRS. LEON WEISSEL. PHOTOGRAPH BY CHARLES KLAMKIN)

153

Fig. 210 The Panama Canal, started during Theodore Roosevelt's administration, was finally finished during Wilson's. This advertising plate, celebrating the accomplishment, has portraits of all the presidents of the United States up to and including Wilson. (MR. AND MRS. LEON WEISSEL. PHOTOGRAPH BY CHARLES KLAMKIN)

home to sip tea from china cups banded in gold with "Votes for Women" embossed in the rim (see Figure 207).

A somewhat less dignified ceramic object representing the difficult struggle for suffrage is a bisque figurine of the black activist suffragette Sojourner Truth. She wore corsets and little else in the suffragette marches. Today the figurine is rarely seen. Although one might think otherwise, it was evidently not meant to be a caricature but a true likeness of Sojourner on the march.

Warren Harding made a mess out of his administration, and he did not live to finish out his term. After his death his name was spoken by many with less than the usual respect given to deceased presidents. The job was too much for Harding, and critics felt he had done the country a favor by dying—especially when details of his private life were revealed. Harding drank, gambled, and kept a mistress during his term of office. He had also fathered an illegitimate child before his nomination. The men to whom he had given jobs in the government betrayed him and the discovery of the Teapot Dome scandals six months after Harding's death verified the fact that the president had been incompetent. Harding had proved that the only true qualification he had for the job of president was that he looked like a president.

Fig. 211 Calvin Coolidge was not a man to be easily caricatured. This redware bank is a good likeness. Legend, "Do as Coolidge does, SAVE," is incised on base. (MR. AND MRS. LEON WEISSEL. PHOTOGRAPH BY CHARLES KLAMKIN)

Fig. 212 Above Glazed intaglio portrait tile of Coolidge's profile. (MR. AND MRS. LEON WEISSEL. PHOTOGRAPH BY CHARLES KLAMKIN)

Fig. 213 Left Hoover toby pitcher with signature on base was made in limited edition. (DEWITT COLLECTION, UNIVERSITY OF HARTFORD. PHOTOGRAPH BY CHARLES KLAMKIN)

155

Calvin Coolidge neither looked like a president nor acted like one. The Vermont-born farm boy got his start in politics in Northampton, Massachusetts, where he served two terms in the Massachusetts House of Representatives. He was voted governor of that state in 1918.

Coolidge received national attention when he was reelected governor of Massachusetts by a landslide. Although he was pushed for the presidency in 1920, Warren Harding chose him as his running mate. Coolidge was a quiet man and drew little attention to himself during his term of office under Harding. "Silent Cal" was sworn into office by his father, in Plymouth, Vermont, while home on vacation. Harding did not leave Coolidge a very pleasant legacy; but try as they would, the Democrats could not implicate Coolidge in the Harding scandals and Coolidge was nominated in his own right for the presidency in 1924, with Charles D. Dawes as his running mate. John W. Davis was the Democratic choice and Robert LaFollette, a liberal from Wisconsin, headed the Progressive party. Coolidge won the election with a popular plurality of 2½ million over the other two major opponents' votes combined.

Coolidge's calm personality and dignified manner could not easily be parodied in clay. A redware bank (Figure 211) with the legend "Do as Coolidge does . . . Save" is really a remarkably dignified likeness of the president, who was well known for being parsimonious. The intaglio tile in Figure 212 is also a dignified portrait of Calvin Coolidge.

Al Smith had a difficult man to beat for the presidency in 1928. Herbert Clark Hoover was an educated, intelligent man who was widely traveled and well read. The basic philosophies of the two men were completely opposite. Hoover believed in the power and innate goodness of big business, whereas Smith believed in social responsibility. Business interests were uppermost in Hoover's dealings, but Smith realized the dangers of letting people be ruled by money interests. Smith had spent a great part of his career fighting for social reforms, and while neither man could have stemmed the terrible economic crisis of 1929, it is more than probable that Al Smith would have dealt with the problems that ensued in a more realistic fashion. It was not the time in American history for the people to choose a mining engineer as their president.

Despite their wide differences as opposing presidential candidates, Hoover and Smith had one thing in common: They both came from very humble beginnings, and both knew what it was like to be poor as children. The difference was that Hoover, by the time he was forty, had accumulated four million dollars.

Ironically, Herbert Hoover won his election on a prosperity ticket. He had been extremely successful in revitalizing the Commerce Department as secretary under Warren G. Harding. "General prosperity," he said during the campaign, "is on my side." The prosperity was to last only seven months. Hoover's management of the country in adversity is, of course, history.

The ceramic toby-mug relics of the Hoover-Smith campaign depict a laughing Smith but a rather serious Herbert Hoover. Perhaps the modeler knew something at the time that the rest of the country would take longer to find out.

Probably one of the most colorful of the also-rans to have been commemorated in earthenware was Alfred E. Smith. Smith was the first presidential candidate to come from among the urban poor. He also had the distinction of being the first Irish Catholic to be nominated for the office of the president of the United States. Humble, plain, and self-made, Al Smith was an assemblyman in Albany and then governor of New York. He was well informed concerning government matters and a superb campaigner.

Smith's record of reform in the state of New York brought him national attention, and he was first nominated for the presidency at the Democratic convention in 1920. This was merely a gesture, but it brought him national attention that grew larger in proportions as he continued to pile up accomplishments in the

Fig. 214 Mug with photoengraving of a very young Alfred E. Smith. Smith was, at the time, an assemblyman in Albany. Reverse of mug shows date for which mug was made. Smith was made governor of New York in 1919 and in 1928 was Democratic nominee for presidency. (DR. EDMUND SULLIVAN. PHOTOGRAPH BY CHARLES KLAMKIN)

Fig. 215 A smiling Al Smith is depicted on this cream colored toby mug made around 1928. (DEWITT COLLECTION, UNIVERSITY OF HARTFORD. PHOTOGRAPH BY CHARLES KLAMKIN)

Fig. 216 Ceramic mug shows a confident Al Smith with cigar. His anti-Prohibition campaign brought him many votes, but not enough to win the election. (MR. AND MRS. LEON WEISSEL. PHOTOGRAPH BY CHARLES KLAMKIN)

governor's mansion in Albany. Franklin Delano Roosevelt nominated Smith at the 1924 convention and again Smith's religion and the fact that he was not in favor of Prohibition kept him from being a serious contender. Smith's nomination for the third time was taken seriously, however, and he became the Democratic candidate in 1928. Smith's religion became a national, rather than a party, issue, and Herbert Hoover was elected the thirty-first president of the United States.

Al Smith was not the sort of politician to appease factions who believed in principles that he felt were wrong. He lashed out, during his campaign, against the Ku Klux Klan, the Woman's Christian Temperance Union, and other groups that differed from his liberal viewpoint. He lost states in the South that traditionally had been Democratic and he even lost his own state of New York. Hoover won by a majority of over six million votes. More damaging to Al Smith than the loss of this election was the defection of his protégé, Franklin Roosevelt, at the 1932 convention, where Smith fully believed he would once again lead his party.

22

CARRY NATION, PROHIBITION, FRANKLIN DELANO ROOSEVELT, AND A ROYAL VISIT

Although it has often been said that you can't legislate morality, throughout its history the government of the United States has kept trying. One such attempt was Prohibition, which lasted from January 1920 to December 1933. While it is true that alcoholism had become a widespread problem in the United States by the end of the nineteenth century, national prohibition by constitutional amendment was not the answer.

Enforcement of the law was nearly impossible, and the Volstead Act ushered in an era of crime and corruption that was worse than the most lurid stories told by Woman's Christian Temperance Union members of the evils of "demon rum." Those who were against the amendment argued that it interfered with their personal liberties and those who were for Prohibition argued that the saloon was the ruination of the American family.

Citizens who were ordinarily law abiding made their own bathtub gin and home-brewed wine. Illegal drinking establishments were opened, and while drinking went underground, it was hardly curtailed. The issue of drink had given rise to several antisaloon organizations in the late nineteenth century, and the Volstead Act was largely the result of an army of crusading, self-righteous women who smashed up saloons and other drinking establishments as an avocation. The leader of this crusade was the zealot Carry A. Nation.

Carry started her saloon-busting career in Kansas, after her first husband turned out to be an incurable alcoholic who was unable to stand unsupported

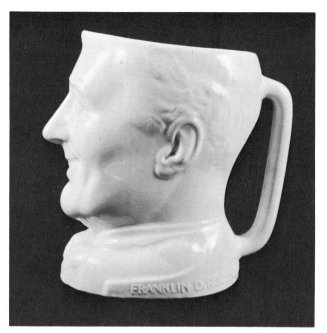

Fig. 217 A young and handsome Franklin D. Roosevelt was the model for this cream colored toby mug. Made as companion to Al Smith mug in figure 182. Roosevelt and Smith, the man he called "The Happy Warrior," eventually became enemies. (DEWITT COLLECTION, UNIVERSITY OF HARTFORD. PHOTOGRAPH BY CHARLES KLAMKIN)

Fig. 218 Early creamware toby mug of Franklin Roosevelt, made before cares of war and depression aged him. (DEWITT COLLECTION, UNIVERSITY OF HARTFORD. PHOTOGRAPH BY CHARLES KLAMKIN)

Fig. 219 "Happy Days Are Here Again" was song that was sung and played during Roosevelt campaign and became associated with Democratic party thereafter. Brown glazed pottery. (DEWITT COLLECTION, UNIVERSITY OF HARTFORD. PHOTOGRAPH BY CHARLES KLAMKIN)

Fig. 220 Campaign mug for Roosevelt era, probably for his first campaign. The New Deal was Roosevelt's plan for improving devastating economic conditions following Hoover administration. Dull yellow glaze on pottery. (DEWITT COLLECTION, UNIVERSITY OF HARTFORD. PHOTOGRAPH BY CHARLES KLAMKIN)

during their wedding ceremony. In her middle and late years, Carry Nation's exploits were followed in the national press, and she became a figure to be reckoned with. Her prejudices were not only against alcohol, but tobacco, sex, the Masonic lodge, and Presidents William McKinley and Theodore Roosevelt.

Mrs. Nation wielded her ax wherever she marched, with a fervor that would put today's women activists to shame. She invited arrest and was frequently accommodated. Thousands of women were inspired to follow Mrs. Nation's example, and while members of her own sex cheered her, many of their husbands debated whether to lynch or to shoot her. Somehow she managed to die of natural causes in Leavenworth, Kansas, on June 2, 1911.

One would hope that the turn-of-the-century dish in Plate 22 is not meant to be an ashtray. It, too, would have been smashed by Carry Nation who hated tobacco. Commemorative plates are sold at the Carry A. Nation home in Medicine Lodge, Kansas. Perhaps they, unlike the small dish illustrated here, have the crusader's name spelled correctly.

Carry Nation did not live to see the Volstead Act passed, but it would have taken more than even women of Mrs. Nation's superstrength to enforce that law. Throughout the period of Prohibition and even before, the subject was a political

*Fig. 221 Another Roosevelt mug, companion to Figure 183, shows happy Democrat in caricature. (*MR. AND MRS. LEON WEISSEL. PHOTOGRAPH BY CHARLES KLAMKIN*)*

Fig. 222 *Souvenir plate with President Roosevelt's portrait in photo-engraving. Probably made during first or second administration.* (MR. AND MRS. LEON WEISSEL. PHOTOGRAPH BY CHARLES KLAMKIN)

Fig. 223 *This plate has engraving of Roosevelt in dignified pose as elder statesman. Probably made around 1940.* (MR. AND MRS. LEON WEISSEL. PHOTOGRAPH BY CHARLES KLAMKIN)

Fig. 224 *Wartime plate showing smiling President Roosevelt amidst scenes of war. Printed on pottery.* (MR. AND MRS. LEON WEISSEL. PHOTOGRAPH BY CHARLES KLAMKIN)

Fig. 225 Creamware bust of Franklin D. Roosevelt was made in extremely limited quantity by Wedgwood and is now rare collector's item. (MR. AND MRS. LEON WEISSEL. PHOTOGRAPH BY CHARLES KLAMKIN)

Fig. 226 Pitcher showing Roosevelt, and Churchill with hat and cigar. (MR. AND MRS. LEON WEISSEL. PHOTOGRAPH BY CHARLES KLAMKIN)

issue. A Prohibition party was organized in 1869, and at its first convention, in Chicago, drew delegates from twenty states. Grover Cleveland was able to win the election in 1884, when the Prohibition party drew important votes from the New York Republicans. Since its organization, the Prohibition party has dwindled in number, but it still hasn't given up entirely.

The Democratic national convention of 1932 demanded repeal of the unenforceable prohibition amendment, and those who had their first legal drink in thirteen years may have toasted the memory of Carry Nation and the future of Franklin Roosevelt in the same alcoholic breath.

There is no question that the country was ready for a strong president by 1933. Campaign promises have a great deal of meaning to a country that has fallen apart at the seams. There was obviously little hope for Herbert Hoover, under whom the economy had reached a low from which it was feared it would never recover.

163

Fig. 227 Blue printed plate to commemorate visit of King George VI and Queen Elizabeth in 1938. (MR. AND MRS. LEON WEISSEL. PHOTOGRAPH BY CHARLES KLAMKIN)

Franklin Delano Roosevelt, crippled by polio, conducted a vigorous campaign in which he covered 27,000 miles and made hundreds of speeches. The strenuous campaign was enough to convince a majority that the Republican-fostered rumors that Roosevelt was physically unfit to take on the burdens of the presidency were unfounded. Roosevelt won the election by a large popular majority and carried all the states but six. His New Deal reforms were put into action immediately following his inauguration on March 4, 1933. He was to continue serving as president for twelve years and forty days.

Although in each of his four campaigns for the presidency, a great deal of campaign material was distributed, very little of the pottery and porcelain Roosevelt relics we find today can be categorized as campaign china. It is probable that the New Deal mug in Figure 220 dates from Roosevelt's first campaign. However, Roosevelt's campaign managers knew the value of spending available campaign funds in media other than china. The radio became an efficient tool for campaign speeches, and other, less expensive objects were made to promote F. D. R. in his first campaign for office. Little campaigning was done for Roosevelt's second, third, and fourth campaigns, and it is likely that the opposition spent a great deal more money in trying to promote their candidates.

164

Fig. 228 Creamware sweet dish made to commemorate visit of king and queen of England in 1939. Legend on reverse side. (JO-ANNE BLUM, INC. PHOTOGRAPH BY CHARLES KLAMKIN)

Creamware mugs, appropriate mementos of the man under whom Prohibition was repealed, can be found with the image of a smiling F. D. R. The commemorative plates of the Roosevelt era depict the president as statesmanlike and dignified. Many other Roosevelt plates were made as memorials following the president's death.

One memorial plate, made by Wedgwood, is still available to collectors. This is a creamware plate in the Edmé shape, with an engraving of Franklin and Eleanor Roosevelt in the center. This design was chosen by Mrs. Roosevelt after the president's death. It was one of four designs offered her by Wedgwood and is currently being sold in the gift shop at Hyde Park (see Figure 230).

Wedgwood also made a creamware bust of Franklin Roosevelt that was never put in full production. A dozen each of two sizes of this bust were made, and scarcity has made this a true collector's item (see Figure 225).

Also illustrated here are two wartime relics (see Figure 224 and Plate 23). One pictures a smiling F. D. R. among prints of planes, ships, parachutists, armed soldiers, guns, and tanks. The legend under the portrait reads "Franklin Delano Roosevelt/President of the United States of America/Supreme Commander of our Armed Forces." The plate is bordered in stars and stripes. The legend on the back of the plate reads:

Fig. 229 Underside of Minton vase (see Plate 23) describing its purpose and showing marks. (AUTHOR'S COLLECTION. PHOTOGRAPH BY CHARLES KLAMKIN)

Fig. 230 Creamware plate by Wedgwood with engraving of Franklin and Eleanor Roosevelt. Chosen by Mrs. Roosevelt to be sold at Hyde Park. (HYDE PARK GIFT SHOP. PHOTOGRAPH BY CHARLES KLAMKIN)

THE UNITED STATES—IN ACTION/December 8, 1941, 12:30 P.M., at joint session of Congress, which was the first war address after the attack on Pearl Harbor. "With confidence in our armed forces—with the unabounding determination of our people—we will gain the inevitable triumph—so help us God."

The plate is a first edition made in 1942 by Vernon Kilns.

Another wartime commemorative of the Roosevelt era is the pitcher in Figure 226 showing portraits of Roosevelt and Winston Churchill surrounded by the flags of England and the United States. The Statue of Liberty is in the center, and the legend "The Champions of Democracy" is written in a banner below the portraits. Churchill is pictured in a typical, although rather undignified, pose. He is wearing a hat and smoking a cigar. On another Roosevelt-Churchill relic, a plate, the prime minister of Great Britain is bareheaded and has put his cigar aside. The double portrait has an oncoming battleship in the center, and the legend below the portraits, printed in sepia, reads "For Democracy" (see Plate 25). On still another wartime plate, a portrait of Roosevelt in sepia is surrounded by all of the flags of the Allies, in color (see Plate 23).

Famous people who have visited the United States have often been immortalized on pottery and porcelain. This tradition, which started with the visit of General Lafayette in 1824, continued into this century. The manufacture of souvenir plates and other pottery or porcelain objects to commemorate a noted visitor, usually royalty, is only possible when the visit is planned long enough in advance to give the enterprising potters time to manufacture and distribute their goods. In these days of jet plane travel, visits do not require long advance notice, and this type of commemorative pottery has become a thing of the past.

In June 1939, Queen Elizabeth and King George VI of England came to America, visited the Roosevelts at the White House, attended the World's Fair in New York, and spent a week-end with the President and Mrs. Roosevelt at their home in Hyde Park, New York.

Both Wedgwood and Minton issued commemorative china in honor of this occasion. Both items were sold in the United States exclusively by Wm. Plummer & Co. of New York. Wedgwood's item was a creamware sweet dish with an embossed border and a profile portrait of King George in blue bas-relief. The American eagle is in blue in the border, with the date 1939 on its shield. The motto "Friendship Makes Peace" surrounds the eagle. The legend on the reverse side of the Wedgwood dish reads:

Commemorating first visit of British Reigning sovereigns to these United States in 1939. Made exclusively for W. H. Plummer & Co. Ltd. New York. WEDGWOOD, Etruria, England. Issue limited to 3000 of which this is 51.

A creamware plate, printed in blue, has a foliage border and portraits of the king and queen on the top. On the bottom is a portrait of Roosevelt. In the center of the plate is a picture of the Capitol in Washington and the Supreme Court Building. This engraving is surrounded by the legend:

To commemorate the visit of their majesties King George VI and Queen Elizabeth to the United States of America . . . June, 1939.

By far the most interesting of all china made specially for the royal visit is a vase issued by Minton, also in a limited edition. The vase is a combination of Art Deco and traditional style. It has a gold embossed border around the top rim in which the year of the visit, 1939, is interspersed with the British royal crown. The handles are gilded lion's heads, and scattered on the body of the vase are gold stars. The shape of the vase is bulbous and it narrows to a gold-striped stem that has wingspread eagles embossed around it. An enameled portrait of the king and queen is the decoration on one side, and the American eagle adorns the other side. "Friendship Makes Peace" is printed on the eagle's shield. This vase was issued in an edition of 3,000 and is probably the most elaborate of any commemorative china ever made. It was sold with certificates establishing the number of each vase in the limited edition. This is also printed on the bottom of the vase. Although Minton has been in the business of making pottery and porcelain since 1793, it is obvious that in 1939 their enamelers were still incapable of decorating a vase with enamel that would not eventually chip. On the specimen illustrated here (see Plate 23), King George's bright blue jacket has already begun to flake off.

23

DESIGNS RELATING TO
HARRY S TRUMAN,
DWIGHT D. EISENHOWER
AND JOHN F. KENNEDY

Few men could have faced the job of president of the United States under the circumstances that placed Harry S Truman in the White House in 1945. At the time there was an entire generation of Americans who had known only one president. A major war was raging, terrible decisions remained to be made, and many of Truman's fellow citizens hardly recognized the name of the man who had been vice president under Roosevelt. Truman, however, had had much experience in American government and proved to be an informed and strong leader.

Truman had not wanted the vice presidential nomination when Roosevelt was nominated for his unprecedented fourth term in office. However, he was Roosevelt's choice and was nominated on the second ballot, edging out supporters of Henry Wallace. He served as vice president only a few short weeks before F. D. R.'s death on April 12, 1945.

Harry Truman's record as a leader capable of making awesome decisions is, of course, well known. He ended World War II by deciding to use the atomic bomb, led us through the Cold War, and coped successfully with labor and government problems at home. The Truman doctrine and the Berlin airlift were two of the important decisions to come out of Truman's first administration. Problems with labor and the first Republican-controlled Congress since 1930 added to the burdens of the president.

When Truman decided to run for a term on his own, the liberal press was discouraging, and the Democratic party was dismayed and depressed over his prospects. Henry Wallace organized a third party, and the southern states, unhappy with Truman's civil rights philosophy, defected and formed the Dixiecrat (States' Rights) party. Truman received his party's nomination and chose Alben W. Barkley as his running mate. The Republicans chose Thomas Dewey of New York to oppose Truman. Truman, short of campaign funds, made a strenuous whistle-stop campaign, speaking wherever people gathered to hear him. The election was close, but Truman was the winner. Dewey was reelected governor of New York following his defeat in the national election. In retrospect, one wonders that any man would have wanted the position of president of the United States during those four years, which saw, among other problems, the McCarthy era and American involvement in the Korean War.

In general, the quality of campaign and commemorative china made as giveaways or for sale as souvenirs declined following World War II. Cheap color

Fig. 231 Thomas E. Dewey, dubbed by Alice Longworth as the "bridegroom on a wedding cake," was the Republican nominee for the presidency in 1944 and 1948. This plate was made after he was reelected to his third term as governor of New York, following his national defeats. (MR. AND MRS. LEON WEISSEL. PHOTOGRAPH BY CHARLES KLAMKIN)

Fig. 232 Sweet dish in blue jasper with white bas-relief has profile portrait of our thirty-third president, Harry S Truman. (PHOTOGRAPH COURTESY OF JOSIAH WEDGWOOD AND SONS LIMITED)

Fig. 233 Campaign ashtray of gray and pink glazed pottery has unbeatable slogan for Dwight D. Eisenhower. (MR. AND MRS. LEON WEISSEL. PHOTOGRAPH BY CHARLES KLAMKIN)

Fig. 234 Small ceramic bust of Eisenhower is really a needle case. The head is removable. Made in Japan and probably a campaign item. (MR. AND MRS. LEON WEISSEL. PHOTOGRAPH BY CHARLES KLAMKIN)

Fig. 235 Tiny ceramic elephants were made in a variety of colors for all Republican candidates in 1940. (DEWITT COLLECTION, UNIVERSITY OF HARTFORD. PHOTOGRAPH BY CHARLES KLAMKIN)

Fig. 236 These two elephants were made for Leverett Saltonstall and Henry Bridges. (DEWITT COLLECTION, UNIVERSITY OF HARTFORD. PHOTOGRAPH BY CHARLES KLAMKIN)

172

Fig. 237 The elephant on this convention souvenir mug had every reason to look happy. Eisenhower was certain to win. (MR. AND MRS. LEON WEISSEL. PHOTOGRAPH BY CHARLES KLAMKIN)

Fig. 238 Wedgwood sweet dish with Eisenhower's rather glum portrait is a commemorative of his presidency and shows him in civilian attire. Blue jasper with white bas-relief. (PHOTOGRAPH COURTESY OF JOSIAH WEDGWOOD AND SONS LIMITED)

lithography as plate decoration was used more frequently, and domestic potters took no pride in turning out plates that portrayed the candidates. Undoubtedly the best-made ceramic souvenir of the Truman administration is a Wedgwood sweet dish in blue jasper with the president's portrait in white bas-relief.

Part of the party that reluctantly nominated Harry Truman in 1947 had really wanted World War II hero Dwight David Eisenhower as their nominee. Eisenhower had refused the honor then, but he accepted a bid from the Republican party in 1952, and he was nominated as a candidate for the presidency on the first ballot. Richard Milhous Nixon was chosen as his running mate. Shortly after, Adlai E. Stevenson III was nominated on the Democratic ticket to run against the general-hero.

Eisenhower, with no previous experience in political campaigning, did not wage a very active campaign, and his opponent was a superb orator from a long line of politicians and statesmen. A difficult and embarrassing moment in the campaign occurred when Eisenhower's running mate, Richard Nixon, was accused of accepting money from businessmen to further his political career. In denial, Nixon made his famous "Checkers" speech on nationwide television, flanked by his dog and his wife.

General Eisenhower's campaign style was to remain aloof from all conflicts then confronting the American people: he ignored Senator Joseph McCarthy

173

Fig. 239 Commemorative bust of President Eisenhower. Black basalt. Made by Wedgwood. (PHOTOGRAPH COURTESY OF JOSIAH WEDGWOOD AND SONS LIMITED)

and the terrible issues involved in his "witch hunt," and he spoke in generalities about other important issues. He did, however, promise to end the war in Korea. Eisenhower won the election by a plurality of over six million votes. "I like Ike" was too euphonious a slogan to beat. It is probable that the cheerful little elephant ashtray in Figure 233 is a souvenir from Eisenhower's first political campaign.

The 1956 conventions were almost repeats of the two political conventions four years earlier. The only player who was different was Estes Kefauver, who was nominated by the Democrats for vice president. The election was hardly a close one in any case. Eisenhower won with 457 of a possible 531 electoral votes and a majority of almost ten million popular votes. It's no wonder that the elephant on the 1956 Republican convention souvenir cup (Figure 237) looks so happy. Another campaign souvenir, made in Japan, is a rather Oriental-looking bust of the general in his Eisenhower jacket. Really a needle case, the souvenir has a removable head. The rather overdecorated and gilded plate in Figure 234 was

174

Fig. 240 Small bust of John F. Kennedy is covered with a fake, crackled glaze to make it look old. (MR. AND MRS. LEON WEISSEL. PHOTOGRAPH BY CHARLES KLAMKIN)

Fig. 241 Tile commemorating inauguration of John F. Kennedy, thirty-fifth president of the United States. (MR. AND MRS. LEON WEISSEL. PHOTOGRAPH BY CHARLES KLAMKIN)

Fig. 242 Photoengraved plate of President and Mrs. Kennedy is probably a Washington souvenir item. (MR. AND MRS. LEON WEISSEL. PHOTOGRAPH BY CHARLES KLAMKIN)

175

Fig. 243 China toy figurine of President Kennedy sitting in rocking chair. Figure is in two parts. (MR. AND MRS. LEON WEISSEL. PHOTOGRAPH BY CHARLES KLAMKIN)

Fig. 244 Campaign or souvenir items of presidents made in Japan still depict subjects with oriental features. Small souvenir bust of Kennedy is hardly a good likeness. (MR. AND MRS. LEON WEISSEL. PHOTOGRAPH BY CHARLES KLAMKIN)

Fig. 245 Portrait plate of President and Mrs. Kennedy. Washington souvenir shops were filled with this sort of inexpensive china during the Kennedy administration. (MR. AND MRS. LEON WEISSEL. PHOTOGRAPH BY CHARLES KLAMKIN)

Fig. 246 "In Memoriam" plate of poor quality was probably rushed onto the market shortly after Kennedy's assassination in Dallas in 1963. (MR. AND MRS. LEON WEISSEL. PHOTOGRAPH BY CHARLES KLAMKIN)

undoubtedly made during the period when the Eisenhowers occupied the White House and was probably sold in Washington, D.C., gift shops at that time.

A modern basalt bust (Figure 239) of former President Dwight Eisenhower was issued in 1970 by Josiah Wedgwood and Sons Limited. It was modeled by Donald Brindley and issued in a limited, numbered edition. It is by far the most tasteful ceramic memento of our thirty-fourth president.

During the short term John Fitzgerald Kennedy spent in the White House, manufacturers of cheap souvenir plates and other ceramic objects must have had a field day. Not only were the president and his first lady, Jacqueline, young and popular, they were without a doubt the most attractive and stylish couple ever to occupy 1600 Pennsylvania Avenue. The portrait plates with prints or photo lithographs of the couple (Figures 242, 245) are only two of the many tastelessly commercial items that were made to sell to the millions of tourists who flood Washington, D.C., every year.

John Kennedy, first president of the United States to have been born in the twentieth century, began to campaign for that office long before the Democratic convention of 1960 was held in Los Angeles. His nomination, on the first ballot, had been fought for in primaries across the country. Lyndon Baines Johnson of Texas was chosen as running mate for the Catholic senator from Massachusetts.

Richard Nixon and Henry Cabot Lodge were the Republican candidates whom the Kennedy team had to beat in the November elections, and the campaign was strenuous for both sides. John Kennedy made a vow to visit every state in the country during the campaign, and he was the first presidential candidate to do so. Kennedy, then senator from Massachusetts, had had experience in presidential campaigns. He had worked hard in a vain effort to place Adlai Stevenson in the White House in 1956, even though he himself had lost the vice presidential nomination that year to Kefauver.

The senator's brother, Robert Kennedy, managed the difficult campaign, and the work that had been done in the primaries was helpful in the later campaign. Party leaders such as Harry Truman and Eleanor Roosevelt would not give Kennedy an endorsement at the convention, Truman charging that Kennedy was too young. In truth, at forty-three, Kennedy was only the second youngest president of the United States; Theodore Roosevelt, at forty-two, had been the youngest.

An issue that Kennedy settled early in the campaign was the matter of his religion. He believed, he said, in the separation of church and state. The presence of Lyndon Johnson on the ticket seemed to verify to doubters that this was so.

Whereas General Eisenhower had had the good sense not to debate publicly with Adlai Stevenson, a superb orator and wit, Richard Nixon had less respect for John Kennedy's expertise in public speaking, and he agreed to engage in a series of four television debates with the Democratic candidate during the campaign. Political historians tend to either credit or blame those debates for the Kennedy election in November 1960, depending on which party is theirs. The tile (Figure 240) commemorating John Fitzgerald Kennedy's inauguration as thirty-fifth president of the United States is one of the more artistic Kennedy souvenirs. Certainly, the Japanese-made bisque bust (Figure 244) is one of the least.

Following President Kennedy's fateful trip to Dallas, Texas, on November 22, 1963, the usual plates, plaques, and other souvenir items mourning our fourth martyred president were put on the market. Most of these were in even poorer taste than the early Kennedy souvenir plates (see, for example, Figure 246).

Wedgwood had made a profile jasperware portrait plaque of Kennedy during the president's lifetime, and this, in the form of a sweet dish, is still popular with collectors. In 1971 Wedgwood also introduced a limited edition of 2,000 black basalt busts of John Kennedy (see Figure 248).

Fig. 247 A memorial plate for President Kennedy, in slightly better taste than the one in Figure 211, is printed and rimmed in black. (MR. AND MRS. LEON WEISSEL. PHOTOGRAPH BY CHARLES KLAMKIN)

24

LYNDON B. JOHNSON, ROBERT KENNEDY, AND RICHARD NIXON CHINA

Lyndon Johnson's place on the Democratic ticket in 1960 had been a great help in getting John Kennedy elected, but if Johnson had any designs on the presidency, he certainly had not wanted the office to come to him the way it did. This was obvious to anyone who saw a recently sworn-in bereaved president and his first lady disembark from *Air Force One* following the tragedy in Dallas.

Johnson led the United States during a most difficult time in a way that no other man might. He wasted no time in promoting a civil rights act, declaring his war on poverty, fighting for medical care for the elderly, and announcing an unprecedented tax cut. His Texas life style was unfavorably compared with the more sophisticated ways of the Kennedys, but Johnson's style in handling the Eighty-eighth Congress was strictly his own.

In his partial term of office, before he ran for the presidency in 1964, Lyndon Johnson was continually compared with John Kennedy. His adolescent daughters were less exciting copy for the newspapers and television networks than the Kennedy babies had been, and his first lady would never be the style setter and sophisticated hostess that Jacqueline Kennedy was. A less strong and less well-adjusted family might have become bitter, but the Johnson women seemed capable of living lives as near normal as was possible in the White House.

The one issue that plagued Johnson's term in the White House was the war in Vietnam. While Johnson had inherited this problem from the Truman administration, all the presidents involved before him had refused to escalate the war. The Gulf of Tonkin incident in August 1964 gave Johnson cause to ask for and

Fig. 248 Basalt bust of John F. Kennedy by Wedgwood was made in limited edition of 2,000. (PHOTOGRAPH COURTESY OF JOSIAH WEDGWOOD AND SONS LIMITED)

Fig. 249 This souvenir ashtray showing beer-drinking donkey (printed in red) commemorates a winning occasion in 1964 for Lyndon Baines Johnson. (MR. AND MRS. LEON WEISSEL. PHOTOGRAPH BY CHARLES KLAMKIN)

receive from Congress authority "to take all necessary measures to repel any armed attack against the forces of the United States and to prevent further aggression."

Johnson, who had decided to run for the presidency in 1964, still refused to escalate the war. He chose Hubert H. Humphrey as his running mate in the election. The Republicans' choice for presidential nominee was Barry Goldwater, a conservative Hawk from Arizona. The Johnson-Humphrey ticket won the election by the largest plurality in history (43,129,484 votes to 27,178,188) with the pledge to keep American troops from fighting on Vietnam soil. The subsequent escalation of the war, and Johnson's order to bomb North Vietnam after the terrorist attack on the American military installations at Pleiku in 1965, led to further involvement of American troops in Vietnam and strong criticism of Johnson's war policies from members of both major political parties. Johnson's programs before Congress received less support than previously, and Eugene McCarthy, the liberal senator from Minnesota, announced that he would seek the Democratic nomination in 1968 on the Vietnam issue.

Having lost support from some of his closest friends over the escalation of the war, and unable to bring himself to withdraw totally from what he felt was an honorable commitment, Lyndon Baines Johnson announced on March 31, 1968, that he would not seek reelection.

Eugene McCarthy's strong showing in the New Hampshire primary, prior to L. B. J.'s announcement, prompted Robert Kennedy, brother of the late president, to announce that he would challenge Lyndon Johnson for the Democratic nomination for the presidency in 1968. Johnson's announcement opened possibilities for many presidential hopefuls, but the Kennedy campaign for the primary votes drew a great deal of press attention. Robert Kennedy, campaigning in California for that state's important primary votes, met the same senseless and violent death that had taken his brother.

For the 1968 Republican convention in Miami Beach, Florida, Abercrombie and Fitch, a New York department store, ordered 200 beer mugs with engraved prints of the party emblem, an elephant, from Josiah Wedgwood and Sons Limited, in England (see Figure 251).

The party leader and obvious choice for candidate was Richard Milhous Nixon, the man whom Adlai Stevenson once described as "the kind of politician who would cut down a redwood tree, then mount the stump and make a speech for conservation." Members of his own party seemed to hold Nixon in higher

*Fig. 250 Souvenir plate for Lyndon B. Johnson, probably sold in Washington shops during his administration. (*MR. AND MRS. LEON WEISSEL. PHOTOGRAPH BY CHARLES KLAMKIN*)*

*Fig. 251 Republican souvenir convention mug was made in limited edition of 200 for Abercrombie and Fitch in New York. It was probably given as favor at a high-level dinner in Miami in 1968. (*PHOTOGRAPH COURTESY OF JOSIAH WEDGWOOD AND SONS LIMITED*)*

esteem, and although he had lost the 1960 election to John F. Kennedy and failed to win an election for governor of California in 1962, he was once again nominated by his party to regain the White House for the Republicans.

Hubert Humphrey, the Democratic party's nominee, went into the campaign tainted with the Johnson Vietnam policy. Even his liberal running mate, Senator Edward Muskie of Maine, could not convince the public that complete withdrawal from Vietnam would be forthcoming if the Democrats were elected. In a country divided by Hawks and Doves, and amid the vociferous rebellion of young people, Richard Nixon promised during his campaign to bring the country back together. At this writing, on the eve of the 1972 presidential nominations, one wonders what the campaign slogans will be this time. It is probable that few of them will be printed on plates. The very permanence of pottery and porcelain might deter either party from investing in objects that bear promises which might come back to haunt them.

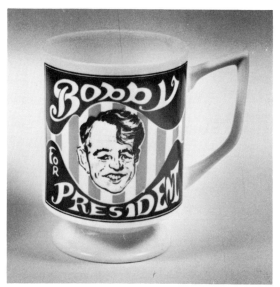

Fig. 252 White ceramic mug was made as primary campaign item before Robert Kennedy's assassination in California in 1968. (MR. AND MRS. LEON WEISSEL. PHOTOGRAPH BY CHARLES KLAMKIN)

Fig. 253 China manufacturers rushed to make a Robert Kennedy memorial plate to be sold in souvenir shops following his death. (MR. AND MRS. LEON WEISSEL. PHOTOGRAPH BY CHARLES KLAMKIN)

25

APOLLO 11 COMMEMORATIVE CHINA

It should be obvious by now that many of the major events, people, places, and symbols that we find on pottery and porcelain made for the American market are a record of 200 years of our history. The ceramics on which our past has been recorded have changed in shape and quality with the passing of time, and their decorations reflect the eras in which they were designed.

These pieces of American patriotic or political china were seldom meant to be fine examples of the potter's art, but rather were objects that could be made quickly and cheaply in great quantities. However, pottery and porcelain objects, although less ephemeral than many other materials on which slogans and opinions can be printed, do break, and objects that were once abundant become scarce and, therefore, more desirable to collectors and historians. The early dark blue and white historical plates that were once abundant in America are now scarce, and the remaining Liverpool jugs that at one time could be found in every seaport town on the East Coast have almost all been purchased by museums or are in private collections.

Campaign plates that were once given away to any willing taker are now carefully collected by those interested in American political history. While it is true that when they were made the pottery plates of the McKinley or Bryan campaigns were far from desirable as quality porcelain, their place in the history of our country makes them as important as the earlier Liverpool ware. The clay used might be different and the methods for printing the message improved, but the potter still leaves the same rather permanent story of American history on every plate and pitcher of a patriotic or political nature.

Fig. 254 Wedgwood plaque commemorating Apollo 11 flight. Blue jasper with white bas-relief.
(PHOTOGRAPH COURTESY OF JOSIAH WEDGWOOD AND SONS LIMITED)

Fig. 255 Dinner service made by Lenox in New Jersey to commemorate the Apollo 11 flight.
(PHOTOGRAPH COURTESY OF LENOX)

Fig. 256 Plates with portraits of all the presidents have been sold in Washington souvenir shops for many years. This plates has portraits of thirty-five presidents. (MR. AND MRS. LEON WEISSEL. PHOTOGRAPH BY CHARLES KLAMKIN)

An American event that would seem to be the least likely subject to be commemorated in the ancient medium of clay is the successful rocket flight to the moon and the landing there of Apollo 11 on July 20, 1969. However, old traditions seem to break through new scientific discoveries, and the accomplishments of the Apollo 11 crew have been commemorated on at least two ceramics manufacturers' products.

A Wedgwood pale blue and white jasper plaque commemorating the Apollo 11 flight was designed and marketed in the United States in 1970. It bears a bas-relief of the space vehicle, the "lem," and the spacemen on the surface of the moon and the legend "Man on the moon/ Apollo 11/ July 20, 1969." The first

Fig. 257 Right In the North during the
Civil War period, it was fashionable to have
shaving mugs decorated with flags that ex-
pressed the sentiment "The Union Forever."
(DEWITT COLLECTION, UNIVERSITY OF HART-
FORD. PHOTOGRAPH BY CHARLES KLAMKIN)

Fig. 258 Below Plate with twenty-seven
presidents' portraits was made during Taft
administration (1909-1913). (DEWITT COL-
LECTION, UNIVERSITY OF HARTFORD. PHOTO-
GRAPH BY CHARLES KLAMKIN).

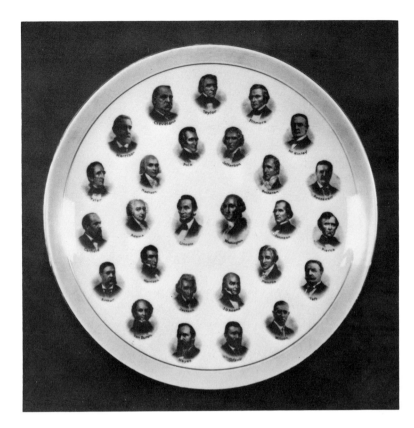

Fig. 259 This less colorful plate was also made during Taft administration, and has twenty-seven Presidents portrayed on it. (DEWITT COLLECTION, UNIVERSITY OF HARTFORD. PHOTOGRAPH BY CHARLES KLAMKIN)

plaque in this edition was presented in London to Captain James A. Lovell of Apollo 8, who was later named to command Apollo 13.

An American ceramics company, Lenox of New Jersey, also made a dinner service commemorating the Apollo 11 trip in 1969. The service plate is decorated with a print of a rather menacing astronaut in a space suit walking on the surface of the moon, with the Apollo 11 insignia in the border. The remainder of the service uses just the border insignia as decoration.

Lenox also created a dinner service that was presented to Commander Walter M. Schirra, Jr., the spaceman from New Jersey who orbited the earth on October 3, 1962. The plates were presented to Commander Schirra on October 15, 1962, at Oradell, New Jersey, by Governor Richard Hughes "on behalf of a people proud of the accomplishments of a native son."

Any important event in our history, it seems, has been the cause for the design and production of a ceramics object to commemorate it. From the landing of the Pilgrims to the landing on the moon, the ancient art of the potter is one medium through which we still record the story of our civilization.

APPENDIX

Commemorative plates made by Josiah Wedgwood and Sons Limited, for Jones, McDuffie & Stratton Co., Boston, Massachusetts, between 1880 and 1900.

Note: All the plates listed are marked "Wedgwood / Etruria / England." Borders feature three large roses interspersed with other flowers.

1. American flag, birth of the, 1777.
2. Arlington, Home of Martha Custis.
3. Boston, The Common and State House, 1836.
4. Boston, Faneuil Hall, 1742.
5. Boston, Green Dragon Tavern.
6. Boston in 1768.
7. Boston, John Hancock, 1737–1863.
8. Boston, King's Chapel, 1686.
9. Boston, Lamb Tavern, 1746.
10. Boston, Old Brick Church, 1713.
11. Boston, Old Corner Book Store.
12. Boston, Old Feather Store, 1680–1868.
13. Boston, Old North Church, 1775.
14. Boston, Old South Church, 1773.
15. Boston, Old State House, East End, 1712.
16. Boston, Old Sun Tavern, 1690–1895.
17. Boston, Old Theater, 1794.
18. Boston, Park Street Church.
19. Boston, Public Library.
20. Boston, State House, 1795.
21. Boston, State Street and Old State House, 1888.
22. Boston Tea Party, 1773.
23. Boston Town House, 1657–1711.
24. Boston, Trinity Church.
25. Bunker Hill Monument, 1843.
26. Cambridge, Washington Elm, 1775.
27. Concord, Mass., Old North Bridge.
28. Grant's Tomb, Riverside Drive, New York.
29. Haverhill, Mass., Birthplace of Whittier.
30. Hingham, Mass., Old Meeting House, 1681.
31. Landing of the Pilgrims, Plymouth.
32. Lexington Common, Battle on, 1775.
33. Longfellow, Birthplace of, Portland, Me.
34. Longfellow's Early Home, 1785, Portland.
35. Longfellow's House, 1843.
36. *Mayflower* in Plymouth Harbor, 1620.
37. *Mayflower*, Return of the.
38. Mount Vernon, 1744–1901.
39. Newburgh, N.Y., Washington's Headquarters, 1750–1899.

40. Niagara Falls.
41. Philadelphia, Independence Hall, 1743–1893.
42. Philadelphia, Signing of the Declaration of Independence, 1776.
43. Pilgrim Exiles.
44. Quincy, Mass., Adjacent Lean-to Houses.
45. Salem, Mass., House of the Seven Gables.

46. Sudbury, Mass., The Wayside Inn, 1683–1899.
47. Washington, Capitol.
48. Washington, Capitol (distant view).
49. Washington Crossing the Delaware.
50. Washington, Library of Congress, 1897.
51. Washington, The White House.
52. Yale College and the Old Yale Fence, New Haven.
53. Yankee Doodle, The Spirit of '76.

The following souvenir plates were issued by Wedgwood in 1900. These were ordered by Jones, McDuffie & Stratton Co. of Boston for special customers.

Note: The border is the same as in the previous list, and the plates are marked on the reverse in the same manner.

1a. Albany, Old State Capitol.
2a. Altoona, Pa., Horse Shoe Curve.
3a. Beverly, Mass., "Hetmere."
4a. California, Carmel Mission.
5a. California, San Fernando Rey Mission.
6a. California, San Gabriel Archangel Mission.
7a. California, San Luis Rey de Francia Mission.
8a. Cleveland, Ohio, Cuyahoga County Soldiers' and Sailors' Monument.
9a. Cleveland, Ohio, Garfield Memorial.
10a. Colorado Springs, Col., The Antlers.
11a. Denver, Col., State Capitol.
12a. Eddy, Home of Mary Baker
13a. Framingham, Mass., Memorial Hall.
14a. Harrisburg, Pa., State Capitol.
15a. Hartford, Conn., First Church.
16a. Holyoke, Mass., Summit House, Mt. Tom.

17a. Lincoln, Neb., State Capitol.
18a. Los Angeles, Cal., Santa Barbara Mission.
19a. Minnehaha Falls, Minnesota.
20a. Mount of Holy Cross, Colorado.
21a. Nantucket, Mass., Old Mill.
22a. New London, Conn., Old Nathan Hale School House.
23a. New London, Conn., Old Town Mill.
24a. Pike's Peak from the Garden of the Gods, Colorado.
25a. Pittsfield, Mass., The Maplewood Hotel.
26a. Pittsfield, Mass., Old Elm Park.
27a. Pittsfield, Mass., Onota Lake.
28a. Pittsfield, Mass., The Wendell Hotel.
29a. Plymouth in 1622.
30a. Portland, Me., State Street Church.
31a. Priscilla and John Alden.
32a. Salem, Mass., First Church.
33a. Salem, Witch House.
34a. Salt Lake City, Utah, Mormon Temple Block.
35a. Springfield, Ill., Lincoln Home.

36a. St. Augustine, Florida, Old City Gateway.

37a. St. Augustine, Florida, Watch Towers of San Moro.

Commemorative plates made for Messrs. Wright, Tyndale, and van Roden of Philadelphia, by Minton, in England, before 1900.

Border designs for all plates in "Geno-vese" pattern show flowers and scrollwork. All plates marked "Minton & Co., England," on reverse. Printed in blue on white earthenware.

1b. Birmingham Meeting House, 1777.
2b. Chester, The Pusey House near (oldest house in Pennsylvania).
3b. Germantown, Chew House, 1777.
4b. Landing of Lafayette, 1824.
5b. Philadelphia, Bartram House.
6b. Philadelphia, Betsy Ross House.
7b. Philadelphia, Carpenters' Hall.
8b. Philadelphia, Christ Church.
9b. Philadelphia, Girard College, 1847.
10b. Philadelphia, Independence Hall, 1743–1901.
11b. Philadelphia, William Penn's Cottage, 1682.
12b. Philadelphia, William Penn's Treaty Tree, 1682.
13b. Philadelphia, Old Swedes' Church, 1697.
14b. Philadelphia, Old Waterworks (Center Square), 1799.
15b. Philadelphia, The Wharton House (scene of Mischianza), 1778.
16b. Radnor, Old St. David's.
17b. Valley Forge, Pa., Washington's Headquarters, 1777–1778.
18b. West Chester, Pa., Old Court House.
19b. Wilmington, Del., Old Swedes' Church.

The following Minton plates have a border called "Lafayette" of small flowers and scrollwork.

20b. Barrat's Chapel (birthplace of Methodism in America).
21b. Birmingham Meeting House, 1777.
22b. Chester, Pa., Old Court House.
23b. Chester, Pa., The Pusey House near.
24b. Germantown, Pa., Old Academy.
25b. Germantown, Pa., Chew House, 1777.
26b. Landing of Lafayette, 1824.
27b. Philadelphia, Bartram House.
28b. Philadelphia, Betsy Ross House.
29b. Philadelphia, Carpenters' Hall.
30b. Philadelphia, Christ Church.
31b. Philadelphia, Girard College, 1847.
32b. Philadelphia, Independence Hall, 1743–1901.
33b. Philadelphia, Sweet Briar.
34b. Philadelphia, William Penn's Cottage, 1682.
35b. Philadelphia, William Penn's Treaty, 1682.
36b. Philadelphia, Old Waterworks (Center Square), 1799.
37b. Philadelphia, The Wharton House (scene of Mischianza), 1778.
38b. Radnor, Pa., Old St. David's.
39b. Stenton, Pa.
40b. Sunbury House on the Neshaminy.
41b. Swarthmore, Pa., The West House.
42b. Valley Forge, Pa., Washington's

Headquarters, 1777–78.
43b. West Chester, Pa., Old Court House.

44b. Wilmington, Del., Old Swedes' Church.

Patriotic designs in dark blue (ca. 1812 to 1830) by Enoch Wood & Sons.

Border: Scroll medallions with inscriptions.

1c. Landing of the Pilgrims.

Border: Seashells, irregular center.

2c. *Cadmus.*
3c. *Cadmus* at Anchor.
4c. *Cadmus* under Full Sail.
5c. *Chief Justice Marshall* (steamboat, Troy line).
6c. Commodore Macdonough's Victory.
7c. *Constitution* and *Guerrière.*
8c. Marine Hospital, Louisville, Ky.
9c. *Union Line* (steamboat, Troy line).
10c. Wadsworth Tower, Connecticut.

Border: Seashells, circular center.

11c. Albany, City of, State of New York.
12c. Baltimore & Ohio Railroad.
13c. Baltimore & Ohio Railroad (inclined plane).
14c. Belleville on the Passaic River.
15c. Capitol at Washington.
16c. Castle Garden, Battery, New York.
17c. Catskill, Hope Mill.
18c. Catskill House, Hudson.
19c. Catskills, Pass in the.
20c. Catskills (Palisades, river, and steamboat).
21c. *Chancellor Livingston* (steamboat).
22c. Gilpin's Mills on the Brandywine Creek.
23c. Greensburg, Tappan Zee from Dobbs Ferry.
24c. Highlands, Hudson River.

25c. Highlands at West Point, Hudson River.
26c. Highlands near Newburgh.
27c. Lake George, N. Y.
28c. Mount Vernon, Home of George Washington.
29c. New York Bay.
30c. Niagara Falls from the American side.
31c. Passaic Falls.
32c. Pine Orchard House, Catskills.
33c. Pine Orchard House (distant view).
34c. Ship of the Line in the Downs (vessel with American flag).
35c. Steamship flying American Flag.
36c. Table Rock, Niagara.
37c. Transylvania University, Lexington, Ky.
38c. Trenton Falls, View of (three people on overhanging rock).
39c. Trenton Falls, View of (one man at foot of falls).
40c. Washington, Capitol at.
41c. Washington, White House (cows in foreground).
42c. West Point, Military Academy.

Border: Wreath of large flowers.

43c. Erie Canal, View of the Aqueduct Bridge at Little Falls.
44c. Erie Canal, Aqueduct Bridge at Rochester.
45c. Erie Canal, Entrance into the Hudson at Albany.

Various borders:

46c. Boston, State House.

47c. Franklin's Tomb.

48c. Washington Standing at Tomb, Scroll in Hand.

49c. Washington's Tomb.

A. STEVENSON

Border: Scrolls and flowers.

50c. Hudson and Sacandaga, Junction of the.

51c. New York, Almshouse in the City of.

52c. New York, Almshouse.

53c. New York, Catholic Cathedral.

54c. New York, City Hall.

55c. New York, Church and Buildings Adjoining Murray Street.

56c. New York, Columbia College.

57c. New York, Fort Ganesvoort.

58c. New York from Brooklyn Heights.

59c. New York from Weehawken.

60c. Perry, The Temple of Fame.

61c. Troy from Mt. Ida.

Various borders.

62c. Dutch Church, 1715–1806, Albany.

63c. Lafayette (portrait).

Border: Wreath of small flowers.

64c. Lake George, On the Road to.

65c. New York from Brooklyn Heights.

66c. New York, Governor's Island, View of.

Border: Large roses and other flowers.

67c. Niagara (sheep-shearing scene).

JAMES CLEWS

Border: Festoons containing names of fifteen states.

68c. Custom House (water and shipping).

69c. Distant View of Public Buildings through Vista of Trees (two women in foreground).

70c. English Castle (water and sailing vessel).

71c. Low, Two-story Structure (probably the White House, sheep in foreground).

72c. Three-story Building and Observatory (two fishermen).

73c. Three-story Building and One-story Wing (deer on lawn).

74c. Three-story Flat Roof Building (no figures).

75c. University Building, Six Wings (sheep on lawn).

76c. View of Mount Vernon.

77c. White House (seen from an angle, with sheep in foreground).

78c. White House (water and rowboat, two figures).

Various borders.

79c. Erie Canal at Albany.

80c. Lafayette, Portrait inscribed, "Welcome, Lafayette, the Nation's Guest and our Country's Glory."

81c. Lafayette, Landing of, at Castle Garden, 1824.

82c. Lafayette, same as 81c with inscription on reverse, "J. Greenfield's China Store, No. 77 Pearl Street, New York."

83c. New York Bay.

84c. New York, Almshouse.

85c. New York, City Hall.

86c. New York, Columbia College.

87c. New York from Brooklyn Heights.

88c. New York, Insane Asylum.

89c. Peace and Plenty (shield with American eagle).

90c. "Perry, The Temple of Fame as Introduced in a Print to the Memory of Commodore, by W. G. Wall, Esq."

91c. Pittsfield, Mass., Winter View of.

J. & W. RIDGWAY, "BEAUTIES OF AMERICA" SERIES

Border: Rose-leaf medallions.

92c. Boston, Almshouse.

93c. Boston, Athenaeum.

94c. Boston, Court House.

95c. Boston, Hospital.

96c. Boston, Insane Asylum.

97c. Boston, Octagon Church.

98c. Boston, St. Paul's Church.

99c. Boston. State House.

100c. Charleston, Exchange.

101c. Hartford, Deaf and Dumb Asylum.

102c. Harvard College, Cambridge.

103c. Mount Vernon.

104c. New York, Almshouse.

105c. New York, City Hall.

106c. Philadelphia, Library.

107c. Philadelphia, Pennsylvania Hospital.

108c. Philadelphia, Staughton's Church.

109c. Savannah, Bank.

110c. Washington, Capitol.

JOHN RIDGWAY

111c. Capitol, Washington, D. C. (high steps and balustrade, monument at top, surmounted by eagle).

Note: The above design was reproduced ca. 1900 by J. C. Brown Westhead, Moore & Co.

JOSEPH STUBBS

Border: Flowers, scrolls, and eagles.

112c. Boston, Nahant Hotel near.

113c. Boston, State House.

114c. Highlands, North River.

115c. Hoboken in New Jersey (Stevens' House).

116c. Hoboken in New Jersey (sheep and dogs).

117c. Hurl Gate, East River, View at.

118c. Mendenhall Ferry (Schuylkill River above Philadelphia).

119c. New York, Dr. Mason's Church in the City of.

120c. New York, City Hall.

121c. New York Bay.

122c. Philadelphia, Bank of the United States (first bank built 1795), from engraving by William Birch & Son, 1799.

123c. Philadelphia, Fair Mount.

124c. Philadelphia, Fair Mount (same as 123c with sheep; only found on platters).

125c. Philadelphia Woodlands.

126c. Philadelphia, Upper Ferry Bridge over the River Schuylkill.

S. TAMS & COMPANY

Border: Foliage of trees.

127c. Philadelphia, United States Hotel.

128c. Harrisburg, Pa., Capitol at (from an engraving by J. L. Frederick).

THOMAS MAYER

Border: Sprays of trumpet flowers and marginal stars.

129c. Arms of Connecticut.
130c. Arms of Delaware.
131c. Arms of Georgia.
132c. Arms of Maryland.
133c. Arms of Massachusetts.
134c. Arms of New Jersey.
135c. Arms of New York.
136c. Arms of North Carolina.
137c. Arms of Pennsylvania.
138c. Arms of Rhode Island.
139c. Arms of South Carolina.
140c. Arms of Virginia.
141c. Arms of New Hampshire.

R. STEVENSON & WILLIAMS (MARKS: ''R. S. W.'' OR ''R. S. & W.'')

Border: Oak leaves and acorns.

142c. Baltimore, Exchange.
143c. Boston, Court House.
144c. Boston, Nahant Hotel near.
145c. Boston, Nahant Hotel near (same as 144c without tree).
146c. Boston, State House.
147c. Columbia College.
148c. Harvard College (several buildings).
149c. Harvard College (single building).
150c. Harvard College (different buildings).
151c. New York, American Museum (Scudders).
152c. New York, City Hotel.
153c. New York, Park Theater.
154c. New York, St. Paul's Chapel.
155c. Philadelphia, Waterworks.
Note: In addition, R. Stevenson & Williams produced portrait plates in honor of the opening of the Erie Canal in 1825. These have either one, two, three, or four portraits in the upper border of the plate. Subjects used were Washington, Jefferson, Lafayette, and Clinton. Scenes in center were: Capitol, Washington, D.C. Same, with white edge, Aqueduct at Rochester; Erie Canal at Albany.

RALPH STEVENSON (MARK: ''R. S.'')

Border: Vine leaves.

156c. Battle of Bunker Hill.
157c. Boston, Almshouse.
158c. Boston, Hospital (canal in front).
159c. Boston Hospital (without canal).
160c. Boston, Lawrence Mansion.
161c. Boston, Massachusetts Hospital.
162c. Brooklyn Ferry.
163c. Charleston, Exchange.
164c. New York, Almshouse.
165c. New York, Battery.
166c. New York, City Hall.
167c. New York, Columbia College.
168c. New York, Esplanade and Castle Garden.
169c. New York, Fort Gansevoort.
170c. New York, Fulton Market.
171c. New York, Hospital.
172c. Savannah, Bank.
173c. Washington, Capitol.

WILLIAM ADAMS

Border: Foliage.

174c. Mitchell & Freeman's China and Glass Warehouse, Chatham Street, Boston.

ROGERS

Border: Floral design.

175c. Boston State House (chaise in foreground).

176c. Boston State House (cows in foreground).

177c. Boston State House (nothing in foreground).

E. & G. PHILLIPS

178c. Tomb of Franklin.

Dark blue designs, makers unknown

Border: Large flowers in four groups of two varieties.

179c. Albany, New York.

180c. Baltimore, Maryland.

181c. Buenos Aires, South America

182c. Chillicothe, Ohio.

183c. Columbus, Ohio.

184c. Detroit, Michigan.

185c. Near Fishkill, N. Y.

186c. Hobart Town, N. Y.

187c. Indianapolis, Indiana.

188c. Louisville, Kentucky.

189c. A View near Philadelphia.

190c. Philadelphia (showing Penn's "treaty tree").

191c. Quebec, Canada.

192c. Richmond, Virginia.

193c. Sandusky, Ohio.

194c. District of Columbia, Washington.

195c. Wright's Ferry on the Susquehanna (from an engraving published by Longman, Hurst, Rees, Orme & Brown, London, 1812).

Border: Fruit and flowers.

196c. Baltimore Court House.

197c. Baltimore, Exchange.

198c. Philadelphia, The Dam and Waterworks (stern-wheel boat).

199c. Philadelphia, The Dam and Waterworks (side-wheel boat).

PORTRAIT PLATES IN
DARK BLUE
BY VARIOUS MAKERS

200c. Washington, Jefferson, Lafayette, and Clinton, with Faulkbourn Hall, England (in center), Aqueduct Bridge, Rochester (at base). (*A. Stevenson*)

201c. Washington, Jefferson, Lafayette, and Clinton, with Faulkbourn Hall, England, Entrance of Erie Canal into Hudson, Albany. (*A. Stevenson*)

202c. Washington, Jefferson, Lafayette, and Clinton, with Aqueduct Bridge, Little Falls, Park Theater, New York. (*R. S. W.*)

203c. Washington, Jefferson, Lafayette, and Clinton, with Niagara (sheep-shearing scene), Entrance to Erie Canal, Albany. (*A. Stevenson*)

204c. Washington, Jefferson, Lafayette, and Clinton, with Niagara (sheep-shearing scene). Aqueduct Bridge, Rochester. (*A. Stevenson*)

205c. Washington, Jefferson, Lafayette, and Clinton, with Park Theater, New York. Aqueduct Bridge, Rochester, (*R. S. W.*)

206c. Washington, Jefferson, Lafayette, and Clinton, with Park Theater, New York, Entrance to Erie Canal, Albany. (*R. S. W.*)

207c. Washington, Jefferson, Lafayette, and Clinton, with Park Theater,

New York. Aqueduct Bridge, Little Falls. (*Maker Unknown*)

208c. Washington, Jefferson, Lafayette, and Clinton, with Aqueduct Bridge, Rochester. Entrance to Erie Canal, Albany. (*R. Stevenson & Williams*)

209c. Washington, Jefferson, Lafayette, and Clinton, with Writtle Lodge, Essex. (*A. Stevenson*)

210c. Washington and Jefferson (at top), Capitol, Washington D. C. (in center), Entrance of Erie Canal, Albany (at base). (*R. S. W.*)

211c. Washington and Lafayette, with City Hotel, New York. Aqueduct Bridge, Little Falls. (*Maker Unknown*)

212c. Washington and Lafayette, with City Hotel, New York, Aqueduct Bridge, Rochester. (*Maker Unknown*)

213. Washington and Lafayette, with Capitol, Washington, D. C. Aqueduct Bridge, Little Falls. (*Maker Unknown*)

214c. Washington and Lafayette. (*R. Stevenson & Williams*)

215c. Washington and Clinton, with Boston Hospital, Entrance to Erie Canal, Albany. (*Maker Unknown*)

216c. Washington and Clinton, with Faulkbourn Hall, England. Aqueduct Bridge, Little Falls. (*Maker Unknown*)

217c. Washington and Clinton, with Faulkbourn Hall, England. Aqueduct Bridge, Rochester. (*Maker Unknown*)

218c. Washington and Clinton, with Niagara, Entrance to Erie Canal, Albany. (*Maker Unknown*)

219c. Washington and Clinton, with Park Theater, New York, Aqueduct Bridge, Little Falls. (*Maker Unknown*)

220c. Washington and Clinton, with Park Theater, New York, Aqueduct Bridge, Rochester. (*Maker Unknown*)

221c. Washington and Clinton, with Capitol, Washington, D.C., Entrance of Erie Canal, Albany. (*Maker Unknown*)

222c. Jefferson and Lafayette, with Boston Hospital. Aqueduct Bridge, Rochester. (*Maker Unknown*)

223c. Jefferson and Lafayette, with Covetham, England. (*Probably by Clews*)

224c. Jefferson and Lafayette, with Capitol, Washington, D.C. Aqueduct Bridge, Rochester. (*Maker Unknown*)

225c. Jefferson and Clinton, with Albany, Aqueduct Bridge, Little Falls. (*Maker Unknown*)

226c. Jefferson and Clinton, with Massachusetts Hospital, Boston. Aqueduct Bridge, Rochester. (*Maker Unknown*)

227c. Jefferson and Clinton, with Park Theater, New York. Aqueduct Bridge, Little Falls. (*Maker Unknown*)

228c. Jefferson, with Columbia College, New York, Aqueduct Bridge, Little Falls. (*R. S. & W.*)

Miscellaneous designs in dark blue

Various borders.

229c. American Villa (Border: fruits and

flowers; not really an American view). B. B. & B.

230c. Baltimore Almhouse (floral border).

231c. Baltimore, Masonic Hall.

232c. Boston Harbor (large eagle and shield with distant view of city).

233c *Cadmus* (two ships; trefoil border).

234c. Erie Canal, Entrance of, into the Hudson at Albany.

235c. Erie Canal (DeWitt Clinton eulogy in center; border: canal boats, etc.).

236c. Erie Canal, Aqueduct Bridge, Little Falls, N.Y. Erie Canal, Aqueduct Bridge, Rochester.

237c. Erie Canal at Utica, 1824 (inscription; border: canal boats, etc.).

238c. Fulton's Steamboat (primitive steamboat with tall smokestack).

239c. Hartford, State House.

240c. Harvard University (floral border).

241c. Lafayette (bust, in uniform. Inscribed "General Lafayette, Welcome to the Land of Liberty," vine-leaf border).

242c. Mount Vernon Inscribed "The Seat of the Late Gen'l Washington." (Washington standing beside horse).

243c. New York, Castle Garden (set border: trefoil and knobs).

244c. New York, St. Patrick's Cathedral, Mott Street.

245c. New York Castle Garden (imported by "Peter Morton, Hartford"; trefoil border).

246c. Philadelphia, Masonic Temple.

247c. University of Maryland.

248c. Washington and Lafayette (urn and scroll border).

249c. Washington from Mount Vernon, View of.

AMERICAN DESIGNS IN DARK BLUE WHICH APPEAR MAINLY ON PITCHERS, JUGS, TEAPOTS, ETC. CA. 1812–1830.

250c. Albany, Dutch Church at.

251c. American Heroes (names of Washington, Truxton, Jones, etc.)

252c. Arms of the United States (large eagle, shield, and flowers).

253c. Baltimore, Masonic Hall.

254c. Erie Canal, Views on the.

255c. Lafayette (bust). Inscribed "Welcome, Lafayette, the Nation's Guest."

256c. Lafayette (bust). Inscribed "Welcome to the Land of Liberty."

257c. Lafayette and Washington (in commemoration of Lafayette's visit in 1824).

258c. Mount Vernon, Washington mountted on horse). Inscribed "Washington's Seat."

259c. "Mount Vernon," the Seat of the Late Gen'l Washington" (Washington standing beside prancing horse and groom).

260c. "Prentiss, Henry, Success to, and his Employ. 1789" (floral designs).

Patriotic china in colors other than dark blue made from around 1830 to 1845.

ENOCH WOOD & SONS
(MARKED: E. W. & S.'')

Border: Fruits and flowers

1d. Buffalo, on Lake Erie.
2d. Fairmount Waterworks on the Schuylkill, Philadelphia.
3d. Fishkill, Hudson River, near.
4d. Harvard College.
5d. Natural Bridge, Virginia.
6d. New York from Staten Island.
7d. Niagara Falls.
8d. Pass in the Catskill Mountains.
9d. Shipping Port on the Ohio River, Ky.
10d. Transylvania University, Lexington, Ky.
11d. Trenton Falls.
12d. Washington (U. S. Capitol).

Border: Checkered, overlaid with vines

13d. Eagle on Rock; River, Steamboat, and City in Background. (*Wood.*)

JAMES CLEWS
(''PICTURESQUE VIEWS''
IN VARIOUS COLORS.
COPIED FROM WATERCOLORS
OF HUDSON RIVER SCENERY
BY W. G. WALL).

Border: Birds and flowers.

14d. Allegheny, near Pittsburgh, Pa., Penitentiary in.
15d. Baker's Falls, Hudson River.
16d. Fairmount Waterworks on the Schuylkill.
17d. Fishkill, Hudson River, from.
18d. Fishkill, Hudson River, near.

19d. Fort Edward, Hudson River.
20d. Fort Miller, Hudson River, near
21d. Fort Montgomery, Hudson River.
22d. Hadley's Falls, Hudson River.
23d. Hudson, Hudson River.
24d. Hudson, Hudson River, near.
25d. Hudson River, View on.
26d. Jessup's Landing, Hudson River, near.
27d. Junction of the Sacandaga and Hudson River.
28d. Little Falls at Luzerne, Hudson River.
29d. Newburgh, Hudson River.
30d. New York, Hudson River (view of Governor's Island).
31d. New York from the Bay.
32d. Pittsburgh (*Home, Lark,* and *Nile* steamboats).
33d. Sandy Hill, Hudson River, near.
34d. Troy from Mount Ida, Hudson River.
35d. West Point, Hudson River.

JOHN RIDGWAY

Border: Large Stars in a firmament of small ones. (Marked: "Columbian Star, October 28, 1840," Engraved by Thomas Hordley.)

36d. Log Cabin (end view; two men).
37d. Log Cabin (side view).
38d. Log Cabin (horses and plow).
39d. *Delaware.*

WILLIAM RIDGWAY

Designs in black with no border or light blue with narrow lace or moss border.

40d. Caldwell, Lake George.

41d. Columbia Bridge on the Susquehanna. (From engraving by W. H. Bartless, published in London by George Virtue, 1838.)

42d. Delaware Water Gap, Pa.

43d. Harper's Ferry from the Potomac Side.

44d. Narrows from Fort Hamilton, The.

45d. Peekskill Landing, Hudson River.

46d. Philadelphia, Pennsylvania Hospital.

47d. Port Putnam, Hudson River, View from Ruggles House.

48d. Valley of the Shenandoah from Jefferson's Rock.

49d. Wilkes Barre, Vale of Wyoming.

50d. Washington, View of the Capitol at.

51d. Undercliff, near Cold Spring, N.Y.

RALPH STEVENSON
(MARKED "R. S.")

Border: Lace design.

52d. Erie Canal at Buffalo.

53d. New Orleans (view of city).

W. ADAMS & SONS

Border: Roses in basket.

54d. Catskill Mountain House.

55d. Conway, N. Hampshire, View near.

56d. Falls of Niagara.

57d. Fort Niagara.

58d. Harper's Ferry.

59d. Headwaters of the Juniata.

60d. Humphreys.

61d. Lake George.

62d. Monte Video, Connecticut.

63d. New York (horseman in foreground).

64d. Schenectady on the Mohawk River.

65d. Shannondale Springs, Va.

66d. West Point Military Academy.

67d. White Mountains, N. H.

W. ADAMS & SONS

Border: Medallions containing sailor boy and ship.

68d. New York (view from river).

ADAMS
(MARKED: "W. A. & S.")

Border: Animal medallions and roses.

69d. Columbus (fleet view: Columbus and two companions, six Indians, two caravels, and two boats).

70d. Columbus (fleet view: one companion, three boats).

71d. Columbus (cavalry view: Columbus and attendant, five Indians, four tents).

72d. Columbus (Indian view: standing Indian and seated squaw, vessel in distance).

73d. Columbus (grayhound view: Indian and three dogs, two tents, and boats).

74d. Columbus (hunting view: standing and seated natives, former shooting wild geese).

75. Columbus (pavilion view: two circular tents, three white men, and three Indians).

76d. Columbus (landing view; procession of thirty white men from beach; three large figures of Indians in tree in right foreground).

J. & J. JACKSON

Border: Floral design.

77d. Albany, N. Y.

78d. Battle Monument, Baltimore.

79d. Boston, Hancock House.

80d. Boston, State House.

81d. Catskill Mountain House, N. Y.

82d. Fort Conanicut, R. I.

83d. Fort Ticonderoga, N. Y.

84d. Hartford.

85d. Harvard Hall.

86d. Lake George.

87d. Little Falls, Mohawk River (view of the canal).

88d. Monte Video, Hartford

89d. Newburgh, N. Y.

90d. New Haven.

91d. New Haven, Yale College and State House.

92d. New York, Battery, &c.

93d. New York, Castle Garden.

94d. New York, City Hall.

95d. Philadelphia, Deaf and Dumb Asylum.

96d. Philadelphia, Girard's Bank (from engraving published by C. G. Childs, Philadelphia, 1829).

97d. Philadelphia, The Race Bridge.

98d. Philadelphia, The Waterworks.

99d. Richmond Court House.

100d. Richmond, Virginia, at.

101d. Saugerties, Ironworks at.

102d. Shannondale Springs, Va.

103d. Washington, The President's House.

104d. White Sulphur Springs (town of Delaware, Ohio, 22 miles from city of Columbus).

THOMAS GODWIN (SERIES OF "AMERICAN VIEWS" PRINTED ON BOTH CIRCULAR AND TWELVE-SIDED PLATES.)

Border: Convolvulus and nasturtium.

105d. Baltimore, City of.

106d. Boston and Bunker Hill.

107d. Brooklyn Ferry.

108d. Columbia Bridge, Pennsylvania.

109d. Fort Hamilton, The Narrows from.

110d. Schuylkill Waterworks, Philadelphia.

111d. Utica, N. Y.

112d. Washington, The Capitol.

CHARLES MEIGH ("AMERICAN CITIES AND SCENERY" SERIES)

Border: Moss and small flowers (chickweed).

113d. Baltimore.

114d. Boston, from the Dorchester Heights.

115d. Boston, Mill Dam.

116d. Judson City, N.Y.

117d. Little Falls, N. Y.

118d. New Haven, Yale College.

119d. New York, City Hall.

120d. Schuylkill Waterworks, Philadelphia.

121d. Utica, N. Y.

THOMAS GREEN

Border: Pattern of small, diamond-shaped figures.

122d. William Penn (standing: companion kneeling; two Indians standing).

123d. William Penn (seated: companion

standing; two Indians—man standing, woman kneeling).

124d. William Penn (standing; companion seated, Indian standing, Indian woman reclining).

125d. William Penn (attendant at right, Indian and Indian woman at left—all standing).

126d. William Penn (attendant standing, two Indians—one seated and one reclining).

JOSEPH HEATH & CO.

Border: Floral design.

127d. The Residence of the Late Richard Jordan (also made without border), New Jersey.

128d. Ontario Lake Scenery.

129d. Monterey.

J. & T. EDWARDS

Border: Four steamships; Columbia, Caledonia, Britannia, Acadia. "Boston Mail" series.

130d. Gentlemen's Cabin (four men).

131d. Gentlemen's Cabin (three men).

132d. Ladies' Cabin.

JOHN TAMS

Border: Two marginal lines (only in light blue).

133d. General W. H. Harrison, "Hero of the Thames, 1813."

134d. Henry Clay, "Star of the West."

MELLOR, VENABLES & CO.

Border: Medallions containing the arms of

the states: New York, Pennsylvania, Massachusetts, Virginia, Maryland, etc.

135d. View of Rear of White House, Washington, D.C.

136d. Capitol Buildings of the Different States Represented in Border.

137d. View of Mount Vernon.

138d. Caldwell, Lake George.

139d. Fort Hamilton, N. Y.

140d. Little Falls, N. Y

141d. Washington's Tomb, Mount Vernon.

J. B. (AT LEAST SIX DIFFERENT POTTERS USED THIS MARK)

142d. "Texan Campaign" (Border: trophies of war and peace).

F. M. & CO.
(FRANCIS MORLEY & CO.)

Border: Ships, etc.

143d. American Marine.

G. L. A. & BRO.
(GEORGE L. ASHWORTH & BRO.)

144d. American Marine (large vessel, broadside; made after 1859. Another variety of the same plate was also made with two small sailing vessels, front view).

T. F. & CO.
(THOMAS FORD & CO.)

145d. "America" (eagle with United States shield, standing on globe).

C. C.

(SEVERAL POTTERS USED
THESE INITIALS ALSO.)

Border: *"Catskill Moss"* (marked on reverse).

146d. Boston from Chelsea Heights (from view in *Boston Notions*, 1848).
147d. Kosckiusko's Tomb.
148d. Meredith, N. H.
149d. Washington, Capitol.
150d. Washington's Tomb, Mount Vernon.

DESIGNS MADE IN A VARIETY
OF COLORS IN LATE PERIOD,
AFTER 1830, BY
UNIDENTIFED MAKERS.

151d. Alabama.
152d. Albany (view of city).
153d. Albany, City Hall.
154d. Albany Theater (1824).
155d. American Flag, Liberty Cap, and Flowers.
156d. "America Triumphant," Eagle, olive branch, ship, and anchor.
157d. Arms of the United States (colored by hand and found on both octagonal and circular plates).
158d. Arms of the United States (flow blue or brown on white; stencil border. (*R. Hammersley*)
159d. Boston, Bunker Hill Monument.
160d. Boston, Court House.
161d. Boston, State House.
162d. Constitution of the United States, First Amendment (central inscription; eagle and motto border. Usually called "Antislavery plate").
163d. Same as 161d. (Lovejoy, Martyr, Alton, Nov. 7, 1837).
164d. *Constitution*.
165d. *Constitution* and *Guerrière*, Fight between (copper luster).
166d. Fort Hamilton, The Narrows.
167d. Fort Hudson, N. Y. (yellow).
168d. Fort Niagara (medallion and flower border).
169d. Franklin (flying kite).
170d. "Fulton's Steamboat."
171d. Harrison, W. H. (log cabin)
172d. Harvard College (stencil border with roses).
173d. Little Falls, View of Aqueduct Bridge at.
174d. "Mt. Vernon, Seat of the Late Gen'l Washington."
175d. "Mt. Vernon" (man and horse in foreground).
176d. Merchants' Exchange, New York (ruins).
177d. Mormon (tabernacle in center; names of brethren in border (*J. Twigg & Co.*)
178d. New Orleans, Old Cathedral, "Municipality, No. 1."
179d. New Orleans, Battery.
180d. New York, Coenties Slip, Burning of the (phoenix and engine border).
181d. New York from Weehawken (lace medallion border).
182d. Niagara.
183d. Niagara Falls (large house in foreground).
184d. "Penn's Treaty with the Indians" (from Benjamin West's painting; overglaze print on porcelain).
185d. Pennsylvania (medallion border). (*K. E. & Co.*)
186d. Dumb Asylum (from engraving published by Hinton & Simpkin &

Marshall, London, 1831), Philadelphia.

187d. Primitive Methodist Preachers, 1830. (*Bourne, Nixon & Co.*)

188d. States (chain of thirteen links containing names of states enclosing ship anchor, etc.; vine border, printed in black). (*Wedgwood*)

189d. Thorps and Sprague, Albany, N. Y.

190d. Utica (medallion border), N. Y.

191d. Virginia (monument; floral border).

192d. Washington, Executive Mansion (same border as Dumb Asylum, Philadelphia).

193d. Washington, Capitol at (floral border).

194d. Washington, White House.

195d. Washington Crossing the Delaware, c. 1865. (*H. P. & W. C. Taylor, Philadelphia*)

196d. Washington Memorial (red and green; urn and willow border).

197d. "Washington" (urn bearing name; floral border).

198d. Washington Vase (pearl color or flow blue).

PORTRAIT PLATES
PROBABLY ALL BY
ENOCH WOOD, DAVENPORT,
AND OTHER STAFFORDSHIRE
POTTERS.

199d. Bainbridge. "Avast, boys, she's struck!"

200d. Brown (bust). "Major-Gen. Brown, Niagara" (view of Niagara Falls, naval emblems, etc).

201d. Decatur. "Free Trade, Sailor's Rights."

202d. Hull (bust). "Captain Hull of the *Constitution.*

203d. Jackson, General (colored border).

204d. Jackson. "Hero of New Orleans." (*Wood*)

205d. Jones (bust). "Captain Jones of the *Macedonian*" (view of ship, naval emblems, etc.).

206d. Perry (bust).

207d. Perry (full-length portrait).

208d. Perry. "We have met the enemy and they are ours."

209d. Pike (bust). "Be always ready to die for your country" (naval emblems, etc.).

210d. Lafayette (bust). "Welcome Lafayette, the Nation's Guest and our Country's Glory" (embossed border).

211d. Lafayette and Washington (raised floral border, red and green).

212d. Lafayette and Washington (raised border, splotches of color).

French plate, maker unknown. Cream-color earthenware. Printed in black or in brown and black. Border: Wreaths of fruit. (Made at Creil, France, c. 1830).

213d. Washington (portrait). From painting by Gilbert Stuart.

214d. The Dutch firm of Petrus Regout, Maestricht, Holland, copied in light blue the "Columbian Star" pattern made for William Henry Harrison's campaign in 1840.

American commemorative plates made by Josiah Wedgwood and Sons Limited, for Jones, McDuffie & Stratton Co. in 1931.

1. Harvard plate designed by Professor Kenneth John Conant of the fine arts department. Twelve views of the college in 1930, printed in blue on white earthenware. Floral and fruit border.

2. Bowdoin plate printed in black on white earthenware, with crests of the college and of its founder, John Bowdoin. Border design of pine branches, ivy, and oak. On first edition of plates is verse written by alumnus Henry Wadsworth Longfellow.

3. Mount Holyoke College plates printed in red, with border design of flowers and foliage and college crest at top. Centers are portraits of founders and famous graduates.

4. Twelve center designs depict "entrances" to the University of Michigan. Border designs by Professor Titcomb, based on the Michigan grape. First edition was numbered and autographed by the president of the University.

5. St. Paul's School, Concord, N. H., plates printed in pink. Borders of squirrels, pine cones, oak leaves, and acorns, together with local fruits and flowers. Centers are action scenes such as crew and hockey games. Plates were also issued in underglaze blue.

6. Princeton University plates have border used in early nineteenth century by Mayer, of flowers and foliage. Centers are scenes of Princeton campus in 1931. Twelve scenes printed in blue on white.

7. Wellesley series in creamware, with embossed border of scrolls and oak leaves broken by lattice panels. In center are etchings of various scenes of campus.

8. Smith College, also creamware, has embossed border of Grecian scroll and etchings of campus scenes in center.

9. West Point series printed in blue on white has many motifs in border: the corps crest; drawings of three cadets in uniforms of 1825, 1848, and 1930; arms and equipment from days of the flintlock; and ancient paraphernalia taken from engravings on old West Point diplomas. Various West Point scenes on center of plate. The reverse of each plate bears a vignette of Whistler's "Third Half Hour," done when he was a cadet at the academy.

10. Vassar College plates designed by art students of the college. Fruit and flower borders including daisies to represent Vassar daisy chain. Centers are campus scenes. Printed in blue, rose, mulberry, and green.

11. University of Pennsylvania plates, printed in blue on white with university seal and three cartouches with college buildings engraved in border. Remainder of border is thistle motif. Center views are various units of the university, including Franklin Field.

12. Wesleyan University plates, printed in mulberry, with motifs of Connecticut state flower, the mountain laurel,

against a lattice motif. University seal at top of plate. Centers are buildings and campus foliage.

13. Yale series is divided into three parts, depicting views from three centuries of Yale's life. Blue on white; scalloped border with rose design. First edition Yale plates have a colophon of the Yale Fence on reverse.

14. Denison College (Granville, Ohio) plates have floral border printed in mulberry. Centers are campus scenes.

15. Massachusetts Institute of Technology plates have scroll border adapted from Chinese design. Centers are campus views. Printed in red.

16. Columbia University plates were designed by Francis A. Nelson, an architect. Plate is scalloped hexagonally, and the floral border design is broken by six insets, three small and three large. At the bottom is the university seal surmounted by a king's crown, with the Columbia lion at the left, the Van Am Memorial on the right. Larger medallions depict the three sites of Columbia. Inner border has Columbia motto. Center drawings of campus buildings by Otto R. Eggers.

17. University of California plates with border of cyclorama of Berkley campus in 1930. Inner border of poppies. Center design campus scenes. Plates are decorated in red by process of photoengraving.

GLOSSARY

POTTERY AND PORCELAIN TERMS
USED IN TEXT

ALPHABET PLATES — Plates made, mainly in Staffordshire, England, from 1820 to end of nineteenth century for children, with alphabet embossed or printed around rim and usually transfer decoration in center.

BAS RELIEF — Sculpture in raised relief in which the figures project only slightly from the background. Wedgwood made many portraits of famous Americans by molding the portrait in jasper and applying the portrait to a contrasting color of the clay. This firm is still producing portraits in this manner.

BASALT — Fine-grained, unglazed, black stoneware, made by staining the clay with manganese dioxide. Josiah Wedgwood refined this clay to give it a richer hue, finer grain and smoother surface.

BELLEEK — A fragile, ornamental porcelain of a type originally made in northern Ireland and copied by American ceramics companies in New Jersey and Vermont.

BISQUE — Unglazed ceramic ware which is not meant to be glazed but is hard-fired and vitreous.

BONE CHINA — Hard-fired china whose main ingredient is bones crushed and ground to a powder.

CAMEO — An engraving in relief or intaglio, usually on stone or shell. Similar effect is used in ceramics through the use of molds.

CANEWARE — Tan colored stoneware used by British potters in the eighteenth and nineteenth centuries. Wedgwood refined clays used by previous potters for their buff and brown wares into a lighter body.

CARTOUCHE — French Renaissance motif of an oval or oblong figure with ornamental scrollwork and enclosing motifs or mottoes. Often used in border of plates.

CHINA — A vitreous, transluscent ceramic ware or any porcelain ware. In America, a term used to describe any ware made of pottery or porcelain.

CHINA TOYS — Small figures of animals, people, etc., usually made of inexpensive earthenware or porcelain.

COPPER-ENGRAVING — A design engraved directly by an artist into a polished copper plate. The inked design is then pressed on paper and the paper applied over-glaze to the clay object which has already been fired. The object is further fired and the paper burned off leaving the design on the clay surface.

CREAM-COLORED WARES — See Creamware.

CREAMWARE — Earthenware of ivory or cream color first used by eighteenth century British potters and improved by Josiah Wedgwood.

DELFT — Originally, pottery made in town of Delf (later, Delft) in Holland. Brown pottery with opaque white glaze and painted decoration. Eventually, the term came to mean similar pottery made anywhere, notably in England.

DRABWARE — Ceramic ware invented by Josiah Wedgwood II. Used in smear-glaze or unglazed state, the former having a hard and brittle appearance. Olive-gray in color.

EARTHENWARE — Opaqueware that is porous after the first firing and requires glazing before it can be used in the manufacture of plates or other tableware.

EDMÉ SHAPE — Creamware dinner ware with fluted borders introduced by Josiah Wedgwood and Sons in 1908.

FIGURINE — Small ornamental figure of pottery or porcelain—a statuette.

FLINT ENAMEL WARE — Mottled glaze, usually shades of brown and yellow, often used on earthenware. Resembles tortoise shell. Used extensively on Bennington pottery in the nineteenth century.

FLINT ENAMELED WARE GLAZE — Glassy preparation applied to the surface of bisque graniteware to render it impervious to liquids.

GRANITEWARE — A semivitreous white china somewhat harder than earthenware.

INTAGLIO — Sunken or incised design, the opposite of a cameo. Intaglio portrait tiles, highly glazed, were a particularly successful production of New Jersey and Ohio potters in the second half of the nineteenth century.

JASPERWARE — Dense, white, vitrified stoneware with nearly the same properties as porcelain. When formed thin, it can be translucent. It has a fine, unglazed surface, and the body contains carbonate of baryta. By adding coloring agents, it can be made in a variety of colors and shades but most of the jasper currently being made by Wedgwood for the American market is medium blue with white bas-relief.

LITHOGRAPHY — A means of decorating pottery or porcelain by transferring multicolored designs from stone to paper. Specially oiled inks are used and design is slipped from paper to ceramic object.

LIVERPOOL WARE — Cream colored earthenware with smooth surface made to receive printed over-glaze decoration. So-called because much of this type of ware was shipped from the Staffordshire region of England for decoration in Liverpool. Some of this type of pottery was made in Liverpool as well.

LOWESTOFT — General term given to porcelain made in China for export to the West in the eighteenth and nineteenth centuries. Plates were decorated to Western taste.

LUSTER — An iridescent or metallic film on the surface of ceramicware obtained by the use of metallic oxides, gold, silver, copper, platinum, etc.

MINTON — Staffordshire (England) pottery established in 1793 and continuing until the present day.

MORTARWARE — Extremely hard, vitreous stoneware for the making of mortars, pestles, and other chemicalware. American potters had a difficult time competing with British potters for the sale of this ware.

PARIAN — Hard-paste porcelain produced by casting that resembles Parian marble. Parian was used extensively by nineteenth-century potters—notably Minton and Copeland in England and the United States Pottery in Bennington, Vermont, to produce imitation-marble statuettes and busts.

PEARLWARE — White earthenware body containing a greater percentage of flint and white clay than cream colored ware. A small amount of cobalt is added to the glaze for a still further whitening effect. It was the improvement of this ware by the Wedgwood firm at the end of the eighteenth century that made it possible for other Staffordshire potters to produce cheap blue and white historical plates for the American market.

PLAQUE — A thin flat plate of porcelain or pottery made to hang on the wall, to ornament furniture, to set in jewelry, etc.

PORCELAIN — Translucent, vitrified ware that has been fired at a high temperature.

PORTRAIT MEDALLIONS (or plaques) — Porcelain or pottery plaques on which has been impressed or applied a portrait in bas-relief or intaglio. Portraits are also printed or painted.

POSSET POT — Pot in which to serve a drink made of hot curdled milk with ale, wine, etc., sweetened and spiced.

POTTERY — Soft, lightly fired, opaque earthenware.

QUEEN'S WARE — Earthenware of an ivory or cream color, improved by Josiah Wedgwood.

REDWARE — Hard, fired, usually unglazed stoneware made of red clays.

ROCKINGHAM WARE — A ceramics glaze similar to flint enamel in appearance except that it is usually predominately dark brown in appearance. So-called from similar useful ceramics made in Rockingham, England, with dark glaze.

SCRODDLEDWARE — Name given to American ware made of varicolored clays that have been wedged together to give appearance of marbleized stone. (Also called Agateware.)

STONEWARE — Opaque vitrified body fired at a high temperature and so named because it is excessively hard and practically impervious to water, even without glazing. It is the connecting link between pottery and porcelain.

TOBY MUG (JUG OR PITCHER) — Pitchers or cups made in caricature of fat men. "Toby" was probably the eighteenth-century term for frequenters of ale houses. Nineteenth-century potters made tobies in caricature of well-known faces and figures. This practice continues today.

TORTOISE-SHELL GLAZE — An effect produced in a lead glaze by dusting metallic oxides, such as manganese, cobalt, copper, etc., over the surface of ceramicware.

TRANSFER PRINTING — Art of transferring engraved patterns to the surface of the ware by means of tissue paper and prepared ink.

WEDGWOOD — Term used to describe all ware made by firm of Josiah Wedgwood & Sons, Stoke-on-Trent, Staffordshire, England. Term is used incorrectly by most Americans to describe blue and white jasperware, which is only one of the products made by this company.

WHITEWARE — See Pearlware.

YELLOWWARE — Term used (mainly in America) to describe cream colored ware, which could range in shade from a light ivory to a saffron yellow. The eighteenth-century earthenware made by Staffordshire potters and intentionally glazed bright yellow is called canaryware.

BIBLIOGRAPHY

BARBER, EDWIN ATLEE. *Anglo-American Pottery*. Philadelphia: Patterson and White Company, 1901.

BARRET, RICHARD CARTER. *Bennington Pottery and Porcelain*. New York: Crown Publishers, Inc., 1958.

BURNS, JAMES MCGREGOR. *Roosevelt: The Lion and the Fox*. New York: Harcourt, Brace & World, Inc., 1956.

BUTLER, JOSEPH T. *American Antiques, 1800–1900*. New York: Odyssey Press, 1965.

CAMEHL, ADA WALKER. *The Blue China Book*. New York: Tudor Publishing Co., 1946.

COX, WARREN E. *The Book of Pottery and Porcelain*. New York: Lothrop, Lee & Shepard Co., Inc., 1944.

CUNLIFFE, MARCUS (AND THE EDITORS OF AMERICAN HERITAGE). *The American Heritage History of the Presidency*. New York: American Heritage Publishing Co., Inc., 1968.

DANGERFIELD, GEORGE. *The Era of Good Feelings*. New York: Harcourt, Brace & World, Inc., 1952.

EARLE, ALICE MORSE. *China Collecting in America*. New York: Charles Scribner's Sons, 1892.

EBERLEIN, HAROLD DONALD-SON AND ROGER WEARNE RAMSDELL. *The Practical Book of Chinaware*. Philadelphia: J. B. Lippincott Co., 1925.

EDITORS OF AMERICAN HERITAGE, THE MAGAZINE OF HISTORY. *The American Heritage Pictorial History of the Presidents of the United States*. New York: American Heritage Publishing Co., Inc., 1968.

GODDEN, GEOFFREY A. *An Illustrated Encyclopedia of British Pottery and Porcelain*. New York: Crown Publishers, Inc., 1966.

GODDEN, GEOFFREY A. *British Pottery and Porcelain, 1780–1850*. New York: A. S. Barnes & Company, Inc., 1964.

KANE, JOSEPH NATHAN. *Facts About the Presidents*. New York: Pocket Books, 1964.

MCCAULEY, ROBERT H. *Liverpool Transfer Designs on Anglo-American Pottery*. Portland, Me.: Atheneum Press, 1942.

MANKOWITZ, WOLF AND REGINALD HAGGAR. *The Concise Encyclopedia of English Pottery and Porcelain*. London: André Deutsch, 1957.

METEYARD, ELIZA. *The Wedg-

wood Handbook. (First published in London in 1875). Peekskill, N. Y.: Timothy Trace, 1963.

PRINGLE, HENRY F. *Theodore Roosevelt*. New York: Harcourt, Brace & World, Inc., 1931.

ROOSEVELT, THEODORE. *The Naval War of 1812*. New York: G. P. Putnam's Sons, 1882.

ROSEBOOM, EUGENE H. *A History of Presidential Elections*. New York: The Macmillan Company, 1957.

ROSSITER, CLINTON. *The American Presidency*. New York: Harcourt, Brace & World, Inc., 1956.

SMITH, ALAN. *The Illustrated Guide to Liverpool Herculaneum Pottery, 1796–1840*. New York: Frederick A. Praeger, Inc., 1970.

SMITH, MABEL WOODS. *Anglo-American Historical China*. Chicago: Robert O. Ballou, 1924.

STONE, IRVING. *They Also Ran*. Garden City, N. Y.: Doubleday, Doran & Company, Inc., 1943.

TAYLOR, MRS. ROBERT COLEMAN. *Liberty China and Queen's Ware*. Garden City, N. Y.: Doubleday, Page & Company, 1924.

TAYLOR, ROBERT LEWIS. *Vessel of Wrath: The Life and Times of Carry Nation*. New York: The New American Library, Inc., 1966.

WINCHESTER, ALICE. *How to Know American Antiques*. New York: The New American Library, Inc., 1951.

In addition, various copies of *The Wedgwood Review*, published twelve times a year by Josiah Wedgwood & Sons, Ltd., Barlaston, Stoke-on-Trent, Staffordshire, were used.

Another pamphlet, *Commemorative Plates: Being a Revival in the Early Nineteenth Century Manner*, published jointly by Jones, McDuffie & Stratton Co., Boston, and Josiah Wedgwood & Sons, Ltd., Etruria, England, in 1931, was used.

INDEX